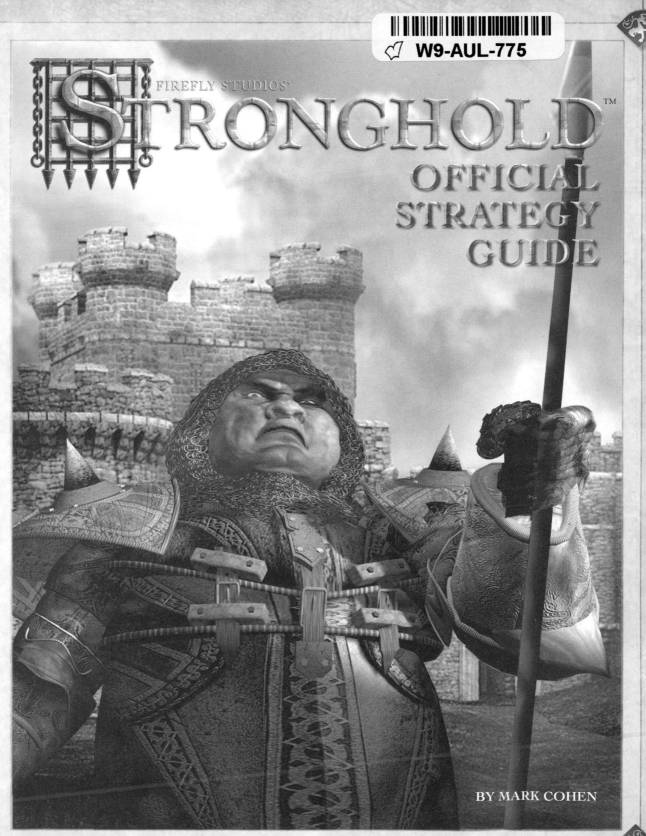

FIREFLY STUDIOS'

Stronghold™

OFFICIAL STRATEGY GUIDE

BY MARK COHEN

STRONGHOLD™
OFFICIAL STRATEGY GUIDE

Brady Publishing

An Imprint of Pearson Education
201 West 103rd Street
Indianapolis, Indiana 46290

ISBN: 0-7440-0104-8

Library of Congress Catalog No.: 2001094879

Printing Code: The rightmost double-digit num-ber is the year of the book's printing; the right-most single-digit number is the number of the book's printing. For example, 01-1 shows that the first printing of the book occurred in 2001.

04 03 02 01   4 3 2 1

Manufactured in the United States of America.

BRADYGAMES STAFF

Director of Publishing
David Waybright

Editor-In-Chief
H. Leigh Davis

Creative Director
Robin Lasek

Marketing Manager
Janet Eshenour

Assistant Licensing Manager
Mike Degler

Assistant Marketing Manager
Susie Nieman

CREDITS

Project Editor
Christian Sumner

Screenshot Editor
Michael Owen

Book Designer
Daniel Caparo

Production Designer
Jane Washburne

BRADYGAMES ACKNOWLEDGEMENTS

BradyGAMES would like to send a special thanks to Jamie Leece, Brian McGinn, Greg Bauman, Simon Bradbury, Eric Ouellette, Michael Best, Robert Thornely, Darren White, Casimir Windsor, and Jorge Cameo.

AUTHOR ACKNOWLEDGEMENTS

I would like to acknowledge several people who provided invaluable assistance on this project. To Editor-In-Chief Leigh Davis of BradyGAMES, thank you for giving me the opportunity to get medieval. To Dan Caparo for designing the guide and capturing the feel of the middle ages. A special thanks to Project Editor Christian Sumner for keeping me moving in the right direction. Once I don the armor and close my helmet, it can be difficult to see the other end of the battlefield. To Darren Thompson and the staff at Firefly, thanks for your help, and a hearty Huzzah! for an incredible simulation. Finally, a special thanks to David Chong for adding his mighty sword to the missions, multiplayer, strategy, and gameplay chapters.

CONTENTS

Chapter 1

WELCOME TO STRONGHOLD

When studying medieval history, many of the images are less than pleasant: stake burnings, horrendous sanitation, rat-infested dungeons, no cable. But, most of us would endure it all (well, maybe not the cable), for a chance to suit up in full armor, grab a sword, and stride around the castle. Unfortunately, we missed our window of opportunity by about 700 years, but the creative team at Firefly Studios spent many long hours in their Keep to bring us Stronghold, the most authentic, historically detailed castle simulation to date. Not just a bash 'em up sword fighting game, Stronghold recreates the economic, social, and military environment of medieval Europe. You can enjoy the game in many ways. When you want action, go straight to Sieges and Invasions, where the catapults and trebuchets start flying within seconds. Or, if you'd rather build gradually to an exciting ending, tackle an Economic or Combat campaign. Of course, the ultimate test of your mettle (and metal) is multiplayer, where you can bump armor with seven other live opponents.

Of course, a game packed with as much detail as Stronghold, needs, and deserves a good strategy guide. We had a great time building, negotiating, and slashing our way through every mission. The end result is a sort of medieval tour book. If you like to read your strategy guides from cover to cover, skip the next section and dive in. You won't be disappointed. However, you might want to spend a few moments and read our chapter preview. This way, when the Pig is tearing down your walls and the peasants are running for cover, you'll be able to quickly find the strategy that will save your kingdom. The following sections include brief chapter summaries, and a few tips on how to use them to your advantage.

GAME BASICS

Stronghold includes an excellent manual, so we do not rehash basic game functions here. However, after playing the game for hours, days, and weeks, we came up with an introductory chapter that is smaller than the manual, but big enough to get you up and running quickly.

THE CHARACTERS OF STRONGHOLD

Once you get past the first few missions of a campaign, your screen is quickly filled with new and interesting characters. They all seem to know where they're going. But do you? In this chapter, we look at every character, giving you a heads up on what they do, why they do it, and how you can improve their lives.

STRUCTURES

Here, we get into the meat of Stronghold. Whether you build a castle or conduct a siege, it all starts with structures that produce the materials you need. In this chapter we profile every structure in the game, from the tallest tower to the tiniest signpost, with critical information on the three "P's": placement, productivity, and protection. You'll come back to this chapter again and again as you learn the rich Stronghold environment.

GENERAL STRATEGIES

This chapter provides some basic guidelines for getting a medieval economy up and running. We show you how to design castles, manage your gold reserves, grow and distribute food, and expand your population. We also provide tips on how to be a "popular" ruler. Of course, you can opt to use gallows and cesspits to motivate your subjects, instead of gardens and churches. But, that's a personal issue we don't have time to address. We'll leave that for your therapist.

After fine-tuning your economy, our military section covers the art of medieval warfare. We provide field-tested strategies for building and maintaining your army, weapons production, castle defenses, deployment and battle tactics, and of course the art of siege warfare. By the time you finish this chapter, you will rule the battlefield.

COMBAT MISSIONS

Now it's time to roll up our chain mail and get into some serious mission walkthroughs. Here you'll find every mission, with tips on meeting your objectives and overcoming some formidable (and nasty) foes. This chapter includes detailed strategies for all combat campaign missions, sieges, and invasions.

ECONOMICS MISSIONS

Here, we cover the economics campaign, individual missions, and free build missions. As in the Combat Mission chapter, you'll find screen shots, tips, warnings, and detailed walkthroughs for every mission.

MULTIPLAYER

After you play every mission (more than 60!), you'll be ready for some live competition. This chapter provides general multiplayer strategies, along with customized tips for all eight multiplayer maps.

MAPS

This section gives an overhead view of the maps that you'll find yourself in. Use these to take advantage of the terrain and come out on top.

Chapter 2

GAME BASICS

Stronghold offers you a wide variety of play modes to satisfy your castle-conquering cravings. All scenarios fall into one of two broad categories: combat missions and economics missions. The combat scenarios, naturally, focus on the siege of a castle. Some of these missions place you in command of the castle garrison, while others task you with invading an enemy stronghold and seizing the keep. The economics missions are completely free of combat, offering specific challenges to your building and management skills. Some even feature time limits on achieving your goals, which can be very hard to meet! Each play mode is described in detail in this chapter, allowing you to choose the one that suits you best.

COMBAT MODES

Playing Stronghold in one of the various combat modes can lead to a wide variety of game experiences. Some of these modes offer individual battles, without any economic considerations. Others feature lengthy scenarios in which you must build a stronghold from the ground up, and then defend it from enemy attack. If you're looking for a clash of steel, one of the combat modes listed below is definitely for you.

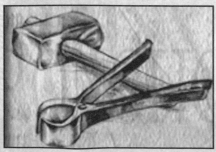

MILITARY CAMPAIGN

The Military Campaign is the centerpiece of Stronghold. This grand saga takes you through an epic series of struggles with the enemies of your king, all nicknamed after unsavory animals. In each mission, you are tasked with raising an army, supporting it with a healthy economy, and repelling one or more enemy attacks on your castle. Some missions begin with a full-fledged stronghold at your command, while others begin with nothing more than a keep and granary. These missions challenge you to use your full suite of economic and military expertise to achieve victory. The campaign missions are collectively the greatest challenge in the game, and players who can conquer it are true Stronghold Lords.

SIEGES

Stronghold allows you the unique opportunity to command the attack or the defense of a large number of historical castles. Can you match the great tactical achievements of history, or avoid the terrible blunders of those who led their troops to destruction? In addition to being an excellent game, Stronghold's historical sieges give you a taste of what it was really like on the battlements of these famous fortresses.

On the defense, you must marshal your troops to the front of your castle as soon as possible. You are assigned a fixed garrison, so you must make the most of what you are given. On the attack, you'll have a few more options open to you. Before the game begins, you can buy and sell troops for your assault force, tailoring it to your preferred style of attack.

INVASIONS

Invasion missions are stand-alone scenarios loosely based upon the events of the combat campaign. They may be played together as a sort of mini-campaign, as well. In most of the Invasion Missions, you are given control of an established stronghold, and you must build up its economy quickly in order to withstand one or more waves of attacks from your enemies. You may be charged with economic goals in addition to the enemy attacks, so be sure to read your mission briefings thoroughly.

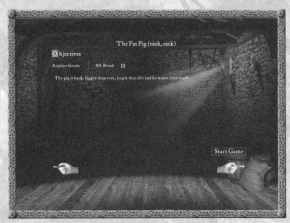

One of the Invasion missions turns the tables by placing you in command of an attacking army. In this case, you must carefully manage your army, conserving your forces for the final assault on the enemy keep. You will not have the opportunity to tailor your forces before the mission, so you must make the best use of what you have.

MULTIPLAYER

Multiplayer games are the ultimate challenge for many players, pitting your skills against those of another thinking, feeling human being. Multiplayer games will unfold much differently than those of the computer opponent, because a human has the tendency to respond emotionally to your actions. Whereas the game's artificial intelligence will always command its forces competently, a human opponent is given to a great range of tactical performance, ranging from horrible blunders to inspired works of military genius. It is your job to capitalize on the enemy's blunders, and save all the genius for yourself.

ECONOMICS MODES

If you're looking to explore the challenges of building and maintaining a Medieval settlement, check out the economics play modes. While these missions don't feature any combat, they are far from easy. You'll be tasked with scratching out an existence in frontier territories, producing vast amounts of goods to satisfy the needs of your king, or building the greatest castle of all time. Certainly, some of the challenges of the economics play modes make fighting a war look like a walk in the park!

Although challenging, most of the economics missions provide you with open-ended timeframes in which to achieve your goals, while remaining free of the threat of enemy attack. As such, you may wish to try playing the economics scenarios before the military scenarios. This will give you the opportunity to master Stronghold's economic system before you have to apply it in times of war.

ECONOMICS CAMPAIGN

The Economics Campaign presents you with a series of challenging scenarios in the service of the king. Each mission is open-ended, so you can take your time learning the various aspects of the Stronghold economy. Also, the campaign introduces the buildings and industries of Stronghold in a gradual progression, so you can learn details of each industry without being overwhelmed.

Each mission challenges you to satisfy a specific set of economic goals. The only way you can really "lose" these missions is to somehow back yourself into an inextricable situation, such as running out of wood without any Woodcutters, or losing all of your population due to unpopularity. Avoid these pitfalls, and you can stick with the mission until you satisfy all of the requirements for victory.

ECONOMICS MISSIONS

You'll find plenty of challenges in Stronghold's Economics Missions. Unlike the campaign, you'll find several missions in this category that hold you to rigid time limits, or force you to come up with creative ways of satisfying your mission goals. Like all economic play modes, the Economics Missions have no enemy attacks in them, so you don't have to worry about providing a defense for your castle. The Economics Missions are an excellent supplement to the campaign, and you'll get the most out of them after you've finished the campaign.

FREE BUILD

Stronghold's Free Build maps allow you to construct the castle of your dreams without fear of enemy attack. You must still manage your economy carefully, and grow at a controlled and methodical pace to avoid running out of any critical resources. Free Build mode is also an excellent way to practice with the interface, or test out the effects of various game elements. Use it to observe the effects of religion on your Popularity, or gauge the number of food workers you need to support a large population.

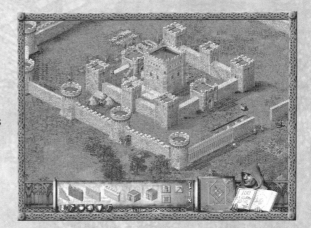

The castles you can create in Free Build mode have the potential to be truly massive. Don't forget to save your games, so you can go back to your favorite castles at any time to add to them, change them, or simply admire your handiwork.

Chapter 3

THE CHARACTERS OF STRONGHOLD

INTRODUCTION

We cover the specific functions of structures in the next chapter, but first, we'd like to introduce the little people of Stronghold. Although the characters of the game are bound by the requirements of their jobs, it is a good idea to know how they move, work, and react. First, a few basics. The unarmed, non-military characters of Stronghold are true pacifists. They will not fight, even if enemy soldiers start swinging their maces or swords. This group includes farmers, pitch diggers, tanners, bakers, and brewers. Your only recourse for protecting these people is to keep them out of harms way. This means locating their places of business behind the castle, out of the way of advancing enemy troops, or placing them within the protection of the castle.

Certain non-military characters happen to carry tools in their job. They will fight to the death, which is usually what happens. This group includes hunters and woodcutters. The most you can expect is that a woodcutter or hunter will be able to kill a few wolves.

However, don't expect any heroics against enemy soldiers.

There are only two, legitimate non-military warriors in Stronghold: the Lord, and the Black Monks. Read on for the glorious details. However, they are certainly the exception, not the rule. For the most part, the characters of Stronghold know their responsibilities, and carry them out through rain, sleet, snow, or siege. Although they never ask you for help, it is up to you to prolong their lives (or make a few more just like them!).

NON-MILITARY CHARACTERS

THE LORD

As we mentioned earlier, the Lord is a force to be reckoned with, either as head of the treasury or protector of his keep. Under normal circumstances, he hangs out atop his keep, or wanders around his castle. For comic relief, he likes to pause and berate soldiers who are lying on the ground. The soldiers keep snoozing, but it seems to make the Lord feel better (it's an anger management thing).

However, when called upon to fight, the Lord is a one-man wrecking crew. He makes short work of wolves or bears, and he can defeat any soldier one-on-one. In fact, he can even hold his own against several Spearmen or Archers. But, he's not invincible. When surrounded, and pounded, his health drops quickly. For this reason, it should be standard operating procedure to surround the Lord with a bevy of bodyguards, preferably Swordsmen, but at the very least, Macemen.

THE LADY

The feminist movement is nowhere to be seen in Stronghold. The Lady of the castle is mostly reclusive, and she appears only briefly, gliding around in her finery. Fortunately, you do not have to dispatch bodyguards to tail her, because enemy soldiers seem to have a "hands off the Lady" policy.

PEASANTS

Peasants come into the world backwards, bowing as they leave the keep. They stroll to the campfire, where they shoot the breeze and wait for job assignments. While lounging in front of the keep, the Peasants are completely vulnerable. They do not fight, and they die very quickly. Despite these humble beginnings, the Peasant is the life-blood of a castle, and without him, there is no hope for your stronghold.

CHILDREN

Children are the tadpoles of Stronghold. They have nothing important to do, so they run around causing mischief and messing up the castle. If you are a benevolent ruler, you can buy them a Maypole and let them swing around in a circle. However, at some point (between diapers and armor), they become Peasants, and finally repay their debt to your society.

MOTHERS AND BABIES

When you place a Hovel, a mother and baby appear, letting you know a family has moved in and Peasants are on the way. Fortunately, they have the good sense to go back to their Hovels when enemy soldiers ransack the castle.

DRUNKARD

Where there's ale, you'll find a drunkard or two. After your Inn starts serving up brews, a couple of tipsy men in green suits wander out of the Inn, bumping into each other, and basically making fools of themselves (wait until you seem them try and negotiate the battlements).

ENTERTAINERS

The Jester runs around acting like a goon, and irritating as many people as possible. Unlike mothers and babies who avoid the battleground, Jesters always seem to end up on the wrong end of a pike. Rounding out the entertainers are the Juggler and Fireater. They provide additional comic relief, and they are always ready to catch enemy arrows. Don't worry, they are self-generating, and will reappear, probably sooner than you'd like.

ENTREPRENEURS

INNKEEPER

One of the most popular people in Stronghold, the Innkeeper keeps the ale flowing. He is accompanied by his trusty dog, and although he loves taking money from the peasants, he knows when to shut his doors. Unfortunately, when he closes up, the Drunkards hit the street.

MARKET TRADER

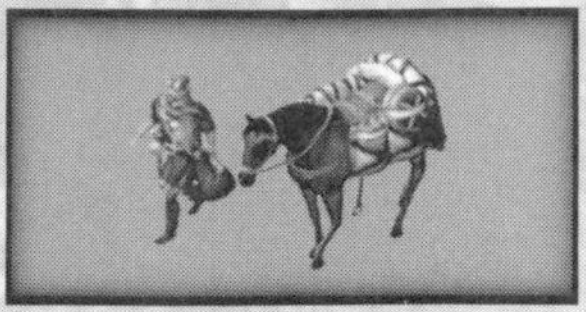

You will see the Market Trader and his horse coming in and out of your castle after you build a Marketplace.

FOOD PRODUCERS

HUNTER

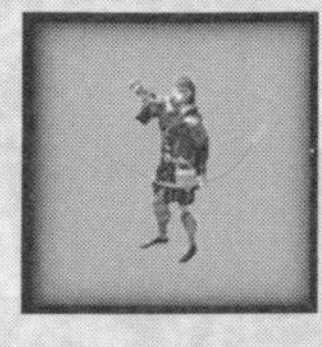

The Hunter is your only option for gathering food early in the combat campaign. However, he is valuable in the later missions when your subjects are hungry, and other food industries take too long to get up and running. The Hunter has the added value of using his bow to kill wolves and bears. He'll even take a pot shot at an advancing enemy soldier, but he is severely overmatched. The Hunter ranges far and wide to chase wild herds, so he has a short lifespan, especially in the later missions.

FARMERS

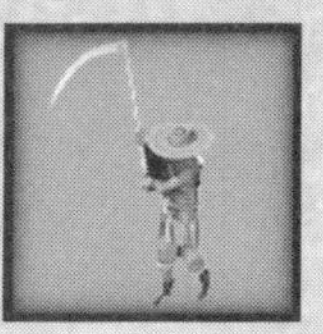

Farmers are hard workers who spend their time working the fields and carrying their produce from the farms to the Stockpile. They take great care in nurturing their crops, so you can make their lives easier by clearing a path to the Stockpile.

MILL BOYS

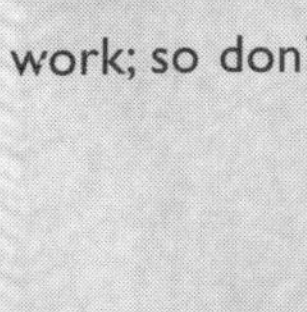

Unlike many workers in Stronghold, the Mill Boys seem to run on high-octane fuel. They carry wheat from the Stockpile to the Mill, where they grind it into flour and carry the sacks back to the Stockpile. They thrive on work; so don't be afraid to build several Bakeries.

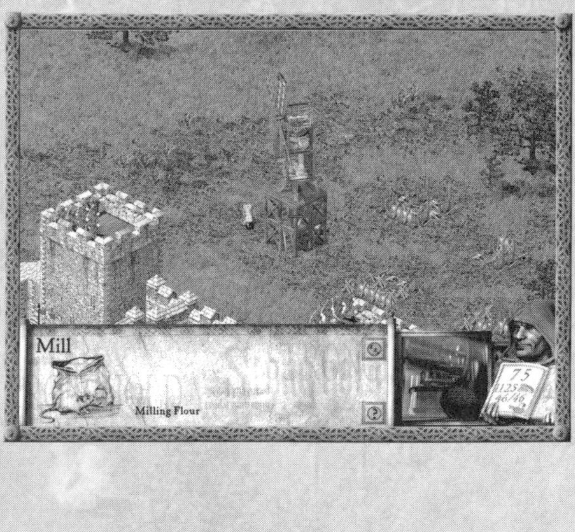

BAKER

If you want to keep plenty of food in the Granary, you'd better hire plenty of Bakers. They take flour from the Stockpile and bake tasty loaves of bread in their busy bakeries.

BREWER

The Brewer keeps the ale flowing, and you will see her carrying bundles of hops to the brewery, and then pushing heavy kegs of ale from the Brewery to the Stockpile. For a good laugh, see if she can push the keg in a straight line, not an easy task after inhaling alcohol fumes all day.

INDUSTRIAL PRODUCERS

WOODCUTTER

The Woodcutter is a burly guy who chops down trees, cuts the timber into planks, and carries eight boards at a time to the Stockpile. Although it is best to place your first Woodcutter's Hut close to a forest, a Woodcutter will scour the map for trees, so there is no need to monitor his progress once he is on the job.

STONE MASON

The Stone Masons work in Quarries where they haul rocks onto a wooden slide and chip them into square blocks. The Drovers then load the blocks onto their Ox Tethers and haul them to the Stockpile. Unfortunately, rock deposits are usually located some distance from the castle, so Stone Masons are very susceptible to attacks.

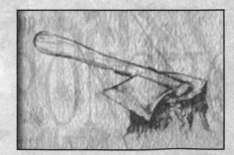

BASICS

CHARACTERS

STRUCTURES

GENERAL STRATEGIES

COMBAT-MISSIONS

ECONOMIC MISSIONS

MULTIPLAYER

MAPS

IRON MINER

Iron Miners are even more isolated than Stone Masons, because ore deposits are frequently found on isolated hilltops. They work in two-man crews. The first miner works deep underground, and then pours the ore into the smelter. The second miner hauls the finished iron bars back to the Stockpile.

PITCH DIGGER

Pitch Diggers have one of the most disgusting jobs in Stronghold. They work on Pitch Rigs that float over oily pools in the swamps. They gather the pitch and pour it into large jars for storage in the Stockpile. The Pitch Diggers are truly unsung heroes to the military, because it is their flaming pitch that can stop a powerful army in its tracks.

DROVER

The Drovers do the legwork for the Stone Masons, loading stone blocks on their Ox Tethers, and driving the load back to the Stockpile.

WEAPON AND ARMOR PRODUCERS

FLETCHER

When you see the Fletcher limping toward the Armory with his latest masterpiece, you know that your army's long-range attack potential just improved. The Fletcher uses wood from the Stockpile to craft bows and crossbows. You can help the Fletcher preserve his one good leg by placing his hut between the Armory and Stockpile.

ARMORER

When you reach the latter stages of the combat campaign, you will depend heavily on the Armorer to outfit your Knights and Swordsmen in shiny protective gear. The Armory fills up quickly in the heavy siege missions, so make sure to leave room for expansion, or your Armorer will be hanging out rather than pounding metal.

BLACKSMITH

The burly Blacksmith forges either maces or swords. Like all of the weapons craftsmen, he hauls completed products to the Armory. The Blacksmith joins the Armorer in fashioning a complete set of gear for Swordsmen and Knights (they also need horses).

POLETURNER

Like the Blacksmith, the Poleturner is responsible for outfitting two types of soldiers, in this case, Spearmen and Pikemen. Wood is his material of choice, and you will need to stay in close contact with the Poleturner to redirect his production priority when battle situations demand new weapons.

TANNER

The Tanner is often a forgotten link in the weapons production chain. Her focus is leather armor worn by Macemen and Crossbowmen. Very unpopular among Dairy Farmers, the Tanner kidnaps cows from the Dairy Farms to provide hides for her armor. You had best add extra farms when Macemen and Pikemen are high on the recruiting list, or your people will miss their daily cheese.

SPIRITUAL GUIDES

PRIEST

This holy man takes residence in a church, chapel, or cathedral, and his calling is to travel far and wide to bless your subjects. He performs weddings, visits new places of business, and often gossips about his flock.

HEALER

When the enemy starts heaving diseased cows into your fortress, you'll be happy to have a Healer on duty. This purple-robed practitioner mixes herbs in his Apothecary, and then rushes to the disease site to dispense remedies to those affected by the spreading cloud of plague.

MILITARY UNITS

Although a strong economy enables you to build a military force, it is your skill as a tactician that determines victory or defeat in most combat missions. You depend on a wide variety of troop classes, from ranged troops like Archers to tough hand-to-hand fighters like Macemen. In this section, we preview each military unit, with tips on how they move and fight. Let's begin with a reference table that summarizes the attributes of each soldier.

Unit	Training Cost (Gold)	Combat Style	Attack Rating (1-5)	Defense Rating (1-5)	Movement (1-5)	Weapon	Armor	Ladder Climbing	Digging Moats
Archers	12	Ranged	2	2	4	Bow	None	Yes	Yes
Crossbowmen	20	Ranged	2	3	3	Crossbow	Leather	No	No
Spearmen	8	Melee	3	2	4	Spear	None	Yes	Yes
Pikemen	20	Melee	3	5	3	Pike	Metal	No	Yes
Macemen	20	Melee	4	3	4	Mace	Leather	Yes	Yes
Swordsmen	40	Melee	5	4	2	Sword	Metal	No	No
Knights	40	Melee	5	4	5	Sword	Metal & Horse	No	No
Tunnelers	30	Melee	3	2	3	N/A	None	No	No
Laddermen	4	N/A	N/A	1	4	N/A	None	No	No
Engineers	30	N/A	N/A	1	3	N/A	None	No	Yes
Black Monks	N/A	Melee	3	3	4	N/A	None	No	No

ARCHERS

The Archer is your bread and butter long-range attack unit. He is most effective against enemy soldiers without armor. Position Archers in towers and turrets, next to Braziers, so they can ignite pitch ditches below. When the fighting moves in close, pull out your Archers before they get worked.

CROSSBOWMAN

Crossbowmen have a shorter range than Archers, but their powerful weapons can penetrate metal armor. Take care not to position Crossbowmen too close to melee troops, because they are slower than Archers, and it takes them longer to reload their weapons.

SPEARMEN

Without armor, the Spearmen are your fastest melee foot-troops. They are also very good at pushing ladders off walls (and they have so much fun doing it!). A squad of Spearmen can rush in and quickly take out Archers, especially if they surprise them from behind. However, their lack of armor keeps them from doing heavy duty against Macemen or Pikemen.

PIKEMEN

Pikemen are the defensive linemen of Stronghold. Only Swordsmen are slower, but the Pikeman's long weapon and heavy metal armor makes him difficult to move out of the way. A line of Pikemen provides serious protection for your Lord.

MACEMEN

Macemen are the thugs of Stronghold. They make short work of most troops in hand-to-hand combat, and they can even knock down walls. However, their leather armor does little to stop arrows, so beware of Archers and Crossbowmen.

SWORDSMEN

It takes time for slow-footed Swordsmen to arrive at the battle, but it's worth the wait. Heavily armored and equipped with a long sword, they easily cut through squads of Macemen and Spearmen. Once you get a force of Swordsmen deep into an enemy castle, they can have their way.

KNIGHT

Horses are scarce, but you would do well to build a large force of Knights. They have it all: power, mobility, and almost impregnable defense. Knights provide the ultimate garrison for your castle, but their speed also makes them valuable on seek-and-destroy missions.

TUNNELERS

These little diggers go deep and tunnel their way underneath a wall or turret. The trick is protecting them while they get close enough to the castle. Nevertheless, once they go underground, destruction is only moments away.

LADDERMEN

Despite poor job security and a short lifespan, the Laddermen are always ready to race to an enemy wall. Follow with ground troops and you can quickly gain entrance to an enemy castle.

ENGINEERS

Engineers build several types of siege engines, and they are not afraid to man the walls when construction is finished. Although their machines are impressive, perhaps their best function is to drop boiling oil on hapless enemy soldiers. They'll complain about carrying the hot pots, but their aim is deadly.

BLACK MONKS

These amazing characters only appear in a couple of missions, where they stand around looking benevolent. However, when the chips are down, they fight like tigers. In fact, they are strong enough to form a protective ring around your Lord.

VILLAINS

Throughout the campaign missions, enemy commanders will plague the strongholds that took you so long to build. The next section contains the biographies of those that want to wipe you from the land. Take advantage of the information and learn your enemy's strengths and weaknesses. Any resources should be taken into account…even information gained through dubious means.

THE RAT

Real Name: Duc de Puce

Age: 20

Height: 5'2"

Weight: Negligible

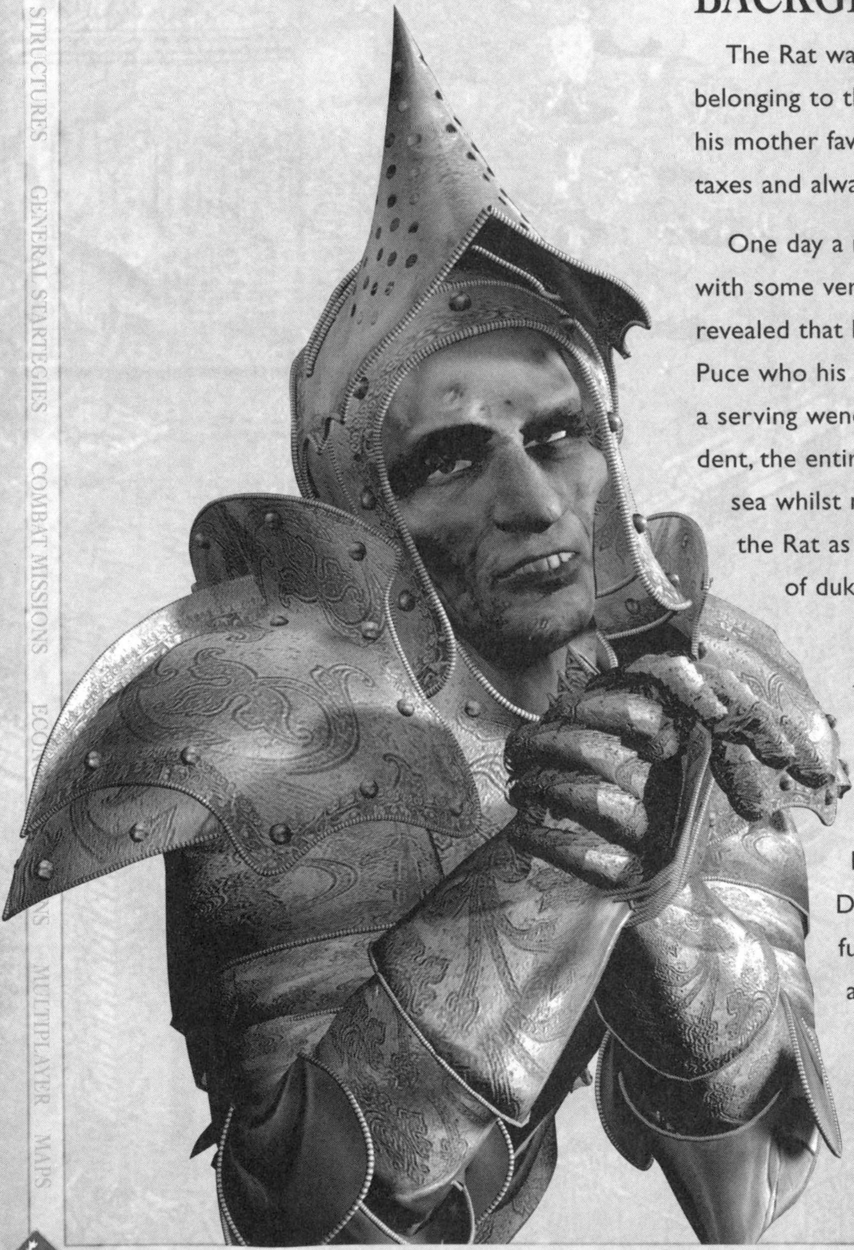

BACKGROUND:

The Rat was raised as an only child in lands belonging to the Puce family. The duke showed his mother favour ensuring that she never paid taxes and always had enough to get by.

One day a messenger came to the door with some very surprising news. It was revealed that his father was the same Duc de Puce who his mother had once worked for as a serving wench. Due to an unfortunate accident, the entire Puce family had been lost at sea whilst returning from holiday leaving the Rat as next in line to inherit the title of duke.

Lacking an education, he turned to Duc Beauregard, who governed a neighbouring province, for advice on how to best manage his lands. More than happy to advise the poor fool, Duc Beauregard sent over a handful of his most loyal staff to assist and, thanks to this aid, the Rat now runs a respectful, if impoverished, kingdom.

APPEARANCE:

Having just turned twenty, the Rat is the scrawniest of enemies to cross your path. This puny weed has been a little late to flower and as such, suffers from an acute acne problem as well having only bum-fluff to loosely cover his fur-lip.

His huge nose and seemingly glued-back pointed ears along with unkempt tufts of hair and large front teeth make him look gaunt and give him his ratty appearance.

The ruffed and regal clothes that he wears are woven from the finest of cloth but are a few sizes too big forcing the Rat to regularly pull his sleeves up and stretch his neck allowing him to speak above his collar.

His sickly pale-green complexion, complete with pus-filled boils adds to the dirty Rat's unhealthy image. It has been rumoured that passers by who look in his general direction often come out in a nasty rash.

PERSONALITY:

The Rat is a highly-strung character with little self-confidence and no capacity to hide this fact. His general jittery nature sometimes gives way to short bursts of spasmodic twitching when he speaks.

His relationship with the rodent world has left him flea-ridden giving him a tendency to scratch himself furiously.

As yet, his voice has not broken and on a few occasions, when threatened, has been known to scream "Eeeak".

His overall skittishness causes him to rapidly look around in different directions when asked for his opinion. When he finally responds, his speech is often splintered with sporadic "errs", "ums" and twitches from his upper lip to fill in the pauses.

To top it all off, the Rat is a poor judge of character making him easy prey for anyone trying to lure the gullible fool into a trap.

THE SNAKE

Real Name: Duc Beauregard

Age: 41

Height: 6'1"

Weight: 9 Stone

BACKGROUND:

The Snake was once made governor to some of the richest provinces in the homeland where he made an extremely fruitful but less than honourable living from under declaring the taxes collected from his people.

The king was eventually made aware of this and decided to have him exiled to Britain in order to keep him at arms length whilst still making use of his talents. Execution was, unfortunately, out of the question as killing such a popular leader with his own hand could well have sparked a revolution.

During one of his first military encounters in Britain he went up against your father, losing an eye to him in a skirmish. On that day the Snake swore he would not rest until the decapitated heads of your entire family were lined-up on spikes outside of his keep.

Already back to his old tricks, the Snake has his greasy hands in the Rats back pocket, draining his coffers with help from the corrupt tax officials initially sent over to give him aid.

APPEARANCE:

Duc Beauregard is a regal looking gent who is relatively tall and of slight build. He is the most elegant of your opponents as well as the best dressed.

His clean-shaven and chiselled face is accentuated by a head of slicked back black hair, which thins to a point at the front. Only the grey flecks above his ears and the few grey hairs in his short, well-groomed black beard betray his age.

As well as wearing tight, figure-hugging clothes, which highlight his slim physique, he also decorates himself with a smattering of lightweight jewellery. The eye patch he wears to conceal his empty socket can make him look menacing at times, however, he usually gives off the confident air of a lovable rogue.

PERSONALITY:

Although the snake is an exceptionally slippery fellow who constantly has his eye open for the next easy profit to be made, this is well hidden behind a confidently worn mask of kindness.

He talks slowly and rhythmically as if being careful not to let his true intensions slip and his voice has a raspy edge that makes him emphasize his "S's".

Always trying to get one-over on whomever he meets, he makes sure to massage the other person's ego whilst smiling confidently with only one side of his mouth when discussions are going well.

If he feels that a deal is about to be struck, he runs his thumb over the pads of his fingers as well as occasionally wetting his lips with rapid flicks of his tongue.

If threatened or antagonised, his voice takes on a more condescending tone and he raises the eyebrow above his good eye as if to accent his disgust.

Overall the snake is a master of the double-cross and will use every dirty trick in the book to stab friends and enemies alike in the back.

THE PIG

Real Name: Duc Truffe

Age: 28

Height: 5'11"

Weight: 20 Stone

BACKGROUND:

When the Pig was born it is rumoured he looked so hideous that his parents abandoned him in the street.

Whatever the case, it is known that he was taken in by a group of travelling bandits who raided small towns and villages throughout the homeland. Whilst growing-up with this small army of rogues he was vastly underfed, however after developing a crude understanding of basic military tactics and being nominated as their leader, the Pig made sure that he had first call on the best foods after each raid and has overcompensated ever since.

After one of the Pig's successful raids, the Wolf paid a visit to his encampment saying he was in search of a leader to command an army and, after seeing the long scar on the Pig's left arm, the Wolf became insistent that he was the right man for the job.

To this day it is still unclear why the Wolf thought the Pig was the best choice or why the king himself agreed with the Wolfs proposition to grant the Pig dukedom but however this came to be, the Pig now runs an effective, if over populated, kingdom.

APPEARANCE:

The Pig is a big fat slobbering mess of a man and by far the least attractive enemy you will encounter. His obesity is so out of hand that he can no longer fully support his own weight and has to walk hunched forwards, but he usually relies on his shire horse 'snowy' whose previous role was to transport slabs of rock up and down mountains.

Although he is relatively tall, the size of his girth coupled with the fact that he has no neck makes him appear stocky.

His piggy appearance comes from his nose which points upwards, complete with a golden ring through the nostrils, along with a pair of large sticky out ears, one of which folds down slightly. Adding to the repulsion, his squat face has a flushed red complexion and an overhanging, furrowed brow mirrors his protruding jaw.

The Pig wears a chain mail vest large enough to house a small peasant family which the Wolf had custom made for him with the Pigs coat-of-arms displayed on the front. The sleeveless vest leaves exposed a scar running from shoulder to elbow on his left arm.

PERSONALITY:

Lacking any concept of etiquette the Pig is usually seen picking his nose or scratching his crotch in plain view of the public. The brute is seldom seen without a cooked animal carcass of some description in one grubby hand and during negotiations he takes delight in ripping off bits of its flesh with his free hand to cram into his mouth.

The Pig rarely speaks unless he is barking an order so may appear to onlookers as less than bright however underestimating him on the battlefield is likely to prove fatal.

As a whole the Pig is a greedy leader who places unreasonable taxes on his people.

CHARACTERS

STRUCTURES

GENERAL STARTEGIES

COMBAT MISSIONS

ECONOMIC MISSIONS

MULTIPLAYER

MAPS

THE WOLF

Real Name: Duc Volpe

Age: 28

Height: 6'4"

Weight: 15 Stone

BACKGROUND:

The Wolf's past is shrouded with mystery and what is known of his history is mainly patched together from stories and unreliable rumours alone. This aside, it is believed that both of his parents died from natural causes in close succession shortly after his eighteenth birthday.

After receiving his dukedom, the Wolf took it upon himself to go travelling, stating he needed some time to think things through, leaving his loyal serfs to manage the lands for him. Nobody knows for certain where he went but he returned a year later with a new companion calling himself the Pig.

After a visit to the king of the homeland himself, he began to instigate his invasion plans of Britain with the Pig in tow as his right hand man.

There have also been wild accusations flying around the kings' court that the Wolf has somehow become involved with the "Order of Black Knights", however there is only unsubstantiated and anecdotal evidence to support these claims.

APPEARANCE:

The Wolf is built from pure muscle, undoubtedly making him the strongest of the foes you will meet. His awesome presence comes mainly from his well-toned gargantuan figure, which is capped with a sturdy pair of broad shoulders.

His square jaw is coated with a layer of rough stubble and, coupled with his well-defined cheekbones, gives him a handsome Germanic look. His pair of cold steely eyes rounded off by thick eyebrows almost meeting in the middle, allow him to turn his intense stare on or off at will.

He usually wears a loose fitting red shirt with the top two buttons undone which exposes his ample chest hair that rhythmically heaves up and down as he breathes.

PERSONALITY:

The Wolf is the cold and calculating master-mind behind the entire saga. Secretive in nature, he gives little away in the form of body language, as he consciously makes sure his arms are folded and eye contact is never severed during negotiations.

His exterior is almost always calm showing a similar amount of emotion as a newly carved stone and even in the face of adversity he manages to keep his cool. Underneath, the cogs never stop whirring as he thinks up the most cunning way to outsmart the opposition.

If someone foolishly antagonises him, he will tense his jaw and slowly circle his neck to release a succession of blood-curdling cracking sounds before retorting.

On the exceptionally rare occasions when he does become enraged, he will curl up one side of his top lip revealing an oversized canine then let out a low growl.

The Wolf is the most efficient as well as the cruellest of leaders rumoured to kill even his most loyal of his staff that step out of line and this causes people under his rule to respect him through sheer terror.

BASICS

CHARACTERS

STRUCTURES

GENERAL STRATEGIES

COMBAT MISSIONS

ECONOMIC MISSIONS

MULTIPLAYER

MAPS

Chapter 4

STRUCTURES

INTRODUCTION

Stronghold is really two games in one: a sophisticated castle builder, complete with a historically accurate economic model; and a medieval military simulation, fully equipped with weapons, fortifications, and units. Choosing the Combat or Economics Campaign allows you to focus on one model. However, it is the blending of both models that gives the player a true medieval experience. At first glance, ale production would not seem to have anything to do with a castle siege. However, when you play "Dealing with the Devil" in the Combat Campaign, you learn that a keg of ale has as much to do with the outcome as a squad of Spearmen.

In this chapter, we organize the Structures of Stronghold into logical groups, based on their common usage. This will help you locate important information quickly when you are in the midst of a heated battle or economic challenge. In addition to reorganizing some of the information that appears in the excellent Stronghold manual, we tunneled into the game engine to bring you a few extra statistics.

CASTLE BUILDINGS

THE KEEP

SAXON HALL	WOODEN KEEP	STONE KEEP	FORTRESS	STRONGHOLD

In every mission of Stronghold, the Keep is the first building you place on the map. The Lord of the castle lives here, and the building also houses the treasury, where you set the kingdom's tax rate. Stronghold includes five different "keeps," beginning with Saxon Hall, which is little more than a large thatched hut. The next level is the Wooden Keep, which is made from tall timbers and it includes an elevated platform. The last three versions, Stone Keep, Fortress, and Stronghold, are all made of stone, and all have raised platforms. Each keep also houses 8-10 Peasants at the beginning of a mission. However, its capacity is limited, and you must build Hovels to accommodate your population as it grows. A keep must be built before you can place a Granary for food storage.

ARMORY

Resource Cost	10 Wood
Workers Required	N/A
Buildings/Materials Required	N/A
Produces/Allows	Weapon and Armor Storage

This is where your weapons are stored. Four different types of weapons are housed in an Armory, with 64 slots. In the advanced combat missions, an Armory fills quickly, so you must allow room for expansion. Unlike other buildings, an additional Armory must be placed adjacent to another Armory. In the interest of production speed, weapons craftsmen like Fletchers, Poleturners, or Tanners should work in close proximity because they must carry the completed weapons from their shops to the Armory.

BARRACKS

Resource Cost	15 Wood or Stone
Workers Required	N/A
Buildings/Materials Required	N/A
Produces/Allows	7 Different Classes of Soldiers

Soldier training takes place in the Barracks. Simply click on the requested troop type to instantly create a soldier. A particular soldier may be created only if you have available Peasants for conscription, and the related weapons and/or armor. As each soldier is created, he appears first at the campfire, and then walks to the Barracks, where all soldiers gather in the training ground. Depending on the mission, Barracks may be constructed of wood or stone.

CASTLE ACCESS POINTS

WOODEN GATEHOUSE

Resource Cost	10 Wood
Workers Required	N/A
Buildings/Materials Required	Woodcutter's Hut
Hit Points	200

This is the least expensive, and correspondingly, the weakest gate in Stronghold. However, the elevated platform is well worth the cost, especially in the early missions when enemy troops are equipped with light weapons. Additionally, a Wooden Gatehouse provides protection from wolves

and bears, while still allowing workers to move in and out of your castle. Even in later missions, a Wooden Gate can serve as an inexpensive access point for areas not threatened by attack, when stone is not available.

> ## Note
>
> Castle Access Points and Defensive Structures add a "Hit Points" rating (except for the Drawbridge). This is a defensive strength rating. A higher number requires more "hits" from attacking troops to bring it to the ground.

SMALL STONE GATEHOUSE (INNER GATE)

	Resource Cost	10 Stone
	Workers Required	N/A
	Buildings/Materials Required	N/A
	Hit Points	1000

Stone has obvious advantages over wood, and the Small Stone Gatehouse provides a secure entry/exit point for your castle. This "Inner Gate" requires less space than the Large Stone Gatehouse, so it is perfect for access to inner courtyards. A defensive-minded castle builder can even entice attacking forces to flow through Inner Gates into an area that is heavily defended.

LARGE STONE GATEHOUSE (MAIN GATE)

	Resource Cost	20 Stone
	Workers Required	N/A
	Buildings/Materials Required	N/A
	Hit Points	2000

This is your main entry to your castle. It is massive in size, offering more resistance to enemy siege engines than the Inner Gate, and you have a higher (and wider) elevated platform for Archers, Crossbowmen, or Engineers armed with Boiling Oil. You can add a Drawbridge to either stone. Gatehouse.

DRAWBRIDGE

	Resource Cost	10 Wood
	Workers Required	N/A
	Buildings/Materials Required	N/A

A Drawbridge is attached to a Gatehouse, providing access over a Moat. The most important consideration when building a Drawbridge, is to place it **before** you dig out the Moat. The Drawbrige has a limited span, and if your Moat is too wide, you'll need to fill it in before the Drawbridge is operational.

CASTLE DEFENSIVE STRUCTURES

WOODEN PLATFORM

Resource Cost	10 Wood
Workers Required	N/A
Buildings/Materials Required	N/A
Hit Points	200

A wooden palisade is made much stronger and more effective with Wooden Platforms. The elevated platform allows bowmen to gain an all-important height advantage over their attackers, be they human or animal. However, keep in mind, the Wooden Platform goes down like a stack of toothpicks when pummeled by Macemen, Spearmen, or Battering Rams. It is important to withdraw your elevated troops **before** the platform tumbles to the ground, or they are surely doomed.

PERIMETER TURRET

Resource Cost	10 Stone
Workers Required	N/A
Buildings/Materials Required	N/A
Hit Points	1000

The smallest of the stone towers, the Perimeter Turret is quite possibly your best defensive expenditure. It must be attached to a wall to provide troop access, so it is best suited to the corners of a castle, or length of wall. Keep in mind, the Perimeter Turret is built on a shallow foundation, so it is especially vulnerable to Tunnelers.

DEFENSE TURRET

Resource Cost	15 Stone
Workers Required	N/A
Buildings/Materials Required	N/A
Hit Points	1200

The Defense Turret holds more troops than a Perimeter Turret, and it is stronger and taller. However, it also requires an attached wall for access, and it is still susceptible to damage from Tunnelers.

SQUARE TOWER

	Resource Cost	35 Stone
	Workers Required	N/A
	Buildings/Materials Required	N/A
	Hit Points	1600

The Square Tower is larger and taller than a Defense Turret, and it has the added capacity to handle a siege weapon, like a Mangonel or Ballista. Square Towers cannot be destroyed by a Tunneler and they can absorb 33% more damage than a Defense Turret.

ROUND TOWER

	Resource Cost	40 Stone
	Workers Required	N/A
	Buildings/Materials Required	N/A
	Hit Points	2000

This is the biggest, strongest (twice as strong as a Perimeter Turret), and most expensive tower in Stronghold. Sieging a castle reinforced with Round Towers is a daunting task, even for an army equipped with Catapults and Trebuchets.

TRAPS AND ENHANCEMENTS

KILLING PIT

	Resource Cost	6 Wood
	Workers Required	N/A
	Buildings/Materials Required	Woodcutter's Hut

The Killing Pit is an inexpensive, hidden trap that is harmful to your enemies, but harmless to your own troops. The effect against heavily armored enemy soldiers, like Swordsmen or Knights, is negligible. For the cost, a Pitch Ditch is more efficient.

PITCH DITCH

	Resource Cost	1 Pitch/4 tiles of Pitch Ditch
	Workers Required	N/A
	Buildings/Materials Required	Pitch Rig

A Pitch Ditch is a perfect way to slow the enemy. Not only does it supply a lot of defense for the cost, but it also works against the more dangerous troops that you'll be facing. It's extremely efficient against armored foot soldiers of all types.

BASICS

CHARACTERS

STRUCTURES

GENERAL STARTEGIES

COMBAT MISSIONS

ECONOMIC MISSIONS

MULTIPLAYER

MAPS

BRAZIER

Resource Cost	N/A
Workers Required	N/A
Buildings/Materials Required	N/A

The Brazier is a small fire lamp that is used to ignite arrows. A flaming arrow does a little more damage than a regular one, but the most important use of the Brazier is to light arrows and fire them at Pitch Ditches. This defensive tactic can set a large area on fire, engulfing the enemy soldiers who are unlucky enough to be walking by. Braziers have no building cost, but they must be placed on castle walls or on towers.

MILITARY BUILDINGS AND WEAPONS

ENGINEER'S GUILD

Resource Cost	10 Wood, 100 Gold
Workers Required	N/A
Buildings/Materials Required	N/A
Produces/Allows	Laddermen and Engineers

The Engineer's Guild is a specialized training facility that produces only Engineers and Laddermen. The cost is 30 Gold for an Engineer and 4 Gold for a Ladderman. For more information, see the Characters chapter.

MANGONEL

Resource Cost	50 Gold
Workers Required	N/A
Buildings Required	N/A
Produces/Allows	Tunnelers

Like the Ballista, the Mangonel must be placed atop a large tower. It is very effective against advancing Spearmen or Macemen. However, like the Trebuchet, a Mangonel is difficult to target. Two Engineers are required for operation.

BALLISTA

Resource Cost	50 Gold
Workers Required	N/A
Buildings Required	N/A
Produces/Allows	N/A

Although technically a siege weapon, the Ballista is not built in the field using an Engineer's tent. It is a large, single-shot arrow launcher that must be placed atop a Square or Large tower. Ballistae are best used targeting enemy siege engines. After a Ballista is built, you must assign two Engineers, or the weapon remains inoperable.

STABLE

Resource Cost	20 Wood, 400 Gold
Workers Required	N/A
Buildings/Materials Required	N/A
Produces/Allows	Horses

A Stable is required to raise horses for your Knights. If you have an available Peasant, horse, and the related armor and weaponry, you can train a Knight.

TUNNELER'S GUILD

Resource Cost	10 Wood, 100 Gold
Workers Required	N/A
Buildings Required	N/A
Produces/Allows	Tunnelers

The Tunneler's Guild produces (duh) Tunnelers. These human moles dig tunnels under towers and walls, and then collapse their tunnels, causing the structures above ground to crumble. If you have an available Peasant, it costs 30 Gold to train one Tunneler. If you click on a Tunneler, he'll tell you he is claustrophobic. Go figure.

OIL SMELTER

Resource Cost	10 Iron, 100 Gold
Workers Required	Engineer needed to operate smelter
Buildings/Materials Required	Pitch
Produces/Allows	Pots of Boiling Oil

The Oil Smelter transforms pitch into boiling oil. An Engineer must be assigned to a smelter. His responsibility is to fill the smelter with pitch from the Stockpile. If you assign additional Engineers to the smelter, they will collect the boiling oil in pots and then wait for assignment. Boiling oil pots are most effective when used from walls, towers, or Gatehouses. After dropping his load of oil, the Engineer must return to the smelter for a refill.

WAR DOG KENNEL

Resource Cost	50 Gold
Workers Required	N/A
Buildings Required	N/A
Produces/Allows	Killer Dogs (4 to a cage)

The War Dogs will not save your castle from a siege, but their presence can be very annoying, for both the enemy and your own troops. Do not release them if friendly soldiers are in the area, because these dogs don't care who they mangle.

SIEGE MACHINES

SIEGE TENT

Resource Cost	N/A
Workers Required	1 or more Engineers to Construct Equipment
Buildings Required	N/A
Produces/Allows	Catapult, Portable Shield, Battering Ram, Siege Tower, Trebuchet

A Siege Tent is an Engineer's field office. After placing a tent, you can select one of the available siege engines for construction. When the Engineer is finished, the tent disappears, leaving the completed engine. Construction is faster when multiple Engineers are involved. For more information on individual siege engine requirements, see the appropriate sections in this chapter.

CATAPULT

Resource Cost	150 Gold	
Workers Required	N/A	
Buildings Required	N/A	
Produces/Allows	N/A	

These mobile rock throwers fire their ammunition at a low trajectory. Their range is somewhat limited, but they can still do considerable damage, especially to unreinforced walls. You can also load Catapults with diseased cattle, and spread the plague behind your enemy's walls. Catapults require two Engineers before they are operational. It is important to remember that a Catapult has limited ammunition (20 rock loads and 3 cows).

TREBUCHET

Resource Cost	150 Gold	
Workers Required	N/A	
Buildings Required	N/A	
Produces/Allows	N/A	

Although not as accurate as a Catapult, Trebuchets can heave large rocks a long way, and when they connect, they do some serious damage. This is the weapon of choice for firing over tall towers and walls. Like Catapults, you can also toss cows, but a Trebuchet requires three Engineers to man the weapon. It comes equipped with enough rocks for 20 throws (like a Catapult), but you get the bonus of five cows, instead of three.

SIEGE TOWER

Resource Cost	150 Gold	
Workers Required	N/A	
Buildings Required	N/A	
Produces/Allows	N/A	

A Siege Tower lets you deposit large squads of soldiers directly onto castle walls. The trick is protecting the vulnerable tower while it gets close enough for the Engineers to extend the gang-plank. It takes four Engineers to operate a Siege Tower.

BATTERING RAM

Resource Cost	150 Gold
Workers Required	N/A
Buildings Required	N/A
Produces/Allows	N/A

These slow-moving behemoths pack a mean wallop, and can bring down a Gatehouse in seconds. If you can protect your Battering Ram during the early minutes of a siege, it is invaluable for smashing through the interior walls of a castle. Like the Siege Tower, it takes four Engineers to operate the Battering Ram.

PORTABLE SHIELD

Resource Cost	5 Gold
Workers Required	N/A
Buildings Required	N/A
Produces/Allows	N/A

When you face waves of enemy Archers, a few well-placed Portable Shields will help your infantry safely cover open ground on their way to the castle. One Engineer is required to operate each Portable Shield.

INDUSTRIAL STRUCTURES

STOCKPILE

Resource Cost	N/A
Workers Required	N/A
Buildings Required	N/A
Produces/Allows	Storage for manufactured and acquired goods, other than Food (Granary), Gold (Treasury), and Weapons (Armory).

Additional Stockpiles must be attached to the original, so you should take care not to overbuild in the surrounding area. If you forget to provide ample storage, you'll receive a voice message during the game. A lack of Stockpile space shuts down every industry that produces items for storage. Brewers will stand around next to their kegs of ale, Woodcutters will sit down on their planks of wood, and Wheat Farmers will hang around the farm with their bundles of wheat. It is better to have a couple empty Stockpiles than to risk running out of space.

WOODCUTTER'S HUT

Resource Cost	3 Wood
Workers Required	1 Woodcutter
Buildings Required	N/A
Produces/Allows	Wood

Wood is the most basic building material in Stronghold, so you can never go wrong with plenty of Woodcutter's Huts. It's always a good idea to place Woodcutter's Huts close to the trees to speed up production time.

QUARRY

Resource Cost	20 Wood
Workers Required	3, and Ox Tether for Hauling
Buildings Required	N/A
Produces/Allows	Stone Blocks

As your castles grow, so does your need for stone. Quarries can only be positioned over light gray boulders, and you may need to search the map for these limited areas. Take your time placing the first Quarry, so you can squeeze the maximum number into a small area.

OX TETHER

Resource Cost	10 Wood
Workers Required	1
Buildings Required	N/A
Produces/Allows	Delivers Stone Blocks to Stockpile

Additional Ox Tethers improve your production time because each one hauls eight blocks at a time to the Stockpile. They can be placed anywhere near the Quarry.

IRON MINE

Resource Cost	20 Wood
Workers Required	2
Buildings Required	N/A
Produces/Allows	Iron

As you advance through the Combat Campaign, iron production becomes critical if you want Swordsmen and Knights in your army. Iron deposits are even harder to find than rock piles. Look for small rust-colored rocks on small hills.

PITCH RIG

Resource Cost	20 Wood
Workers Required	1
Buildings Required	N/A
Produces/Allows	Pitch

Pitch is arguably the most valuable defensive resource in Stronghold. Place your Pitch Rig in the swamps over bubbling oil. The pitch is collected and carried to the Stockpile, where it can be used in Oil Smelters (for boiling oil), or to build pitch ditches, areas in the ground that can be ignited with flaming arrows.

MARKETPLACE

Resource Cost	15 Wood
Workers Required	N/A
Buildings Required	N/A
Produces/Allows	Buying/Selling Goods

If you have more money than food, the Marketplace can make the difference between maintaining your popularity, and inspiring your Peasants to leave for greener pastures. On the flip side, you can also sell surplus goods if your treasury is a little thin. In the advanced missions, you'll need to regularly visit the Marketplace to micro-manage your economy.

FOOD PRODUCING STRUCTURES

HUNTER'S POST

Resource Cost	5 Wood
Workers Required	1
Buildings Required	N/A
Produces/Allows	Meat

Building a few Hunter's Posts is the quickest, least expensive way to get food flowing into your Granary. However, hunters are vulnerable to enemy attack because they must follow the herds of wild animals, wherever they wander. As your community grows, you'll need more diverse sources for food, but it's always comforting to know you can run into the forest and take down a deer when the Granary is empty.

DAIRY FARM

Resource Cost	10 Wood
Workers Required	1
Buildings Required	N/A
Produces/Allows	Cheese

After breeding 3 cows, the dairy farmer begins delivering cheese to the Granary. Under normal circumstances, two Dairy Farms should provide an adequate amount of cheese. However, if your Tanner is taking cows to make leather armor, your cheese production will drop dramatically. Be sure to build several Dairy Farms to support both industries.

APPLE ORCHARD

Resource Cost	5 Wood
Workers Required	1
Buildings Required	N/A
Produces/Allows	Apples

You need fertile valley ground for planting Apple Orchards. It takes time for production to kick into high gear, but your loyal subjects will love the apples, especially when combined with other foods.

WHEAT FARM

Resource Cost	15 Wood
Workers Required	1
Buildings Required	N/A
Produces/Allows	Wheat

Wheat is the stuff of life, and this is especially true in Stronghold. A Wheat Farm is the first step in making bread, when paired with a WindMill for flour production. Wheat has a tendency to rot if left in the field for too long, so make sure to place your farm close to the Stockpile.

HOP FARM

	Resource Cost	15 Wood
	Workers Required	I
	Buildings Required	N/A
	Produces/Allows	Hops

Growing hops is good for what ails your peasants. Combined with a Brewery and Inn, you can boost your popularity level by allowing your peasants to tip a few. Like wheat, hops tend to rot on the vine, so don't make your farmer walk a long way to the Stockpile.

FOOD PROCESSING STRUCTURES

GRANARY

	Resource Cost	10 Wood
	Workers Required	N/A
	Buildings Required	N/A
	Produces/Allows	Food Storage

The Granary not only stores your food, but also tracks how much your subjects are eating. Your people respond to quantity and variety, so if you want to keep your popularity level above 50, pay regular visits to the Granary. You can add additional Granary's as long as they are adjacent to the original one.

BAKERY

	Resource Cost	10 Wood
	Workers Required	I
	Buildings Required	N/A
	Produces/Allows	Bread

If you have a Wheat Farm and Windmill, your baker will have the materials he needs to bake bread. Three or four Bakeries are the staple of any large castle.

WINDMILL

	Resource Cost	20 Wood
	Workers Required	3
	Buildings Required	N/A
	Produces/Allows	Flour

The workers pickup wheat at the Stockpile and take it to the Mill where it is ground into flour. The sacks of flour are then carried back to the Stockpile, where the baker uses it to bake bread.

BASICS

CHARACTERS

STRUCTURES

GENERAL STARTEGIES

COMBAT MISSIONS

ECONOMIC MISSIONS

MULTIPLAYER

MAPS

BREWERY

Resource Cost	10 Wood
Workers Required	1
Buildings Required	N/A
Produces/Allows	Ale

The Brewer takes hops to the Brewery and produces kegs of frothy ale. The kegs end up in the Stockpile, where they are sent to the Inn, sold in the Marketplace, or used to satisfy a mission requirement.

INN

Resource Cost	50 Wood
Workers Required	1
Buildings Required	N/A
Produces/Allows	Distribution

Your people love to unwind with a stein of ale after a hard day in the fields. Every working Inn also rewards you with a popularity boost. However, keep in mind the demand for ale goes up with your population. Therefore, as your settlement grows, you'll need to produce more ale to keep everyone loose and happy.

TOWN BUILDINGS

HOVEL

Resource Cost	6 Wood
Workers Required	N/A
Buildings Required	N/A
Produces/Allows	Housing for 8 Peasants

As your settlement grows beyond its original size, the population will surpass the existing living quarters. Without an empty Hovel, Peasants stop coming to your castle. Simply, build a Hovel to provide room for eight more people. The two upgrades pictured above occur automatically, and do not cost anything. If Hovels are destroyed in battle, the resulting overcrowding will cause an immediate drop in popularity, and eventually, the peasants will leave. You can check your current population and maximum capacity on the scribe's book in the lower right-hand corner of the game screen.

APOTHECARY

Resource Cost	10 Wood, 50 Gold
Workers Required	1
Buildings Required	N/A
Produces/Allows	Disease Prevention

You won't need an Apothecary until enemy armies start heaving diseased cows into your castle. Without a healer to dispense herbs and cure the resulting plague, your peasants will die. If your settlement is very large, you might want to consider two Apothecaries for better coverage.

WELL

Resource Cost	50 Gold
Workers Required	N/A
Buildings Required	N/A
Produces/Allows	Stops Fires from Spreading

Flaming arrows and ignited Pitch Ditches start fires. When the flames burn up enemy troops, it is a good thing. However, fires can spread, and if left unchecked, they can burn up your farms, buildings, soldiers, and citizens. A few strategically placed Wells will stop the fires from spreading beyond their targeted areas.

RELIGIOUS BUILDINGS

CHAPEL

Resource Cost	10 Stone, 250 Gold
Workers Required	N/A
Buildings Required	N/A
Produces/Allows	Priest

CHURCH

Resource Cost	20 Stone, 350 Gold
Workers Required	N/A
Buildings Required	N/A
Produces/Allows	Priest (needed for higher population)

CATHEDRAL

Resource Cost	40 Stone, 500 Gold
Workers Required	N/A
Buildings Required	N/A
Produces/Allows	Priest (needed for very high population)

Your town thrives on religion, and a wandering priest delivers righteousness when he steps out of his Chapel. A place to worship makes your peasants happy. However, a priest can only bless so many people, and when your settlement grows larger, you'll need to add another chapel to handle the load. Pay close attention to messages regarding bigger religious buildings.

LOYALTY CREATORS

Life in a medieval castle is difficult, and a benevolent ruler will reward the peasants with pleasant diversions to their wretched lives. The following "Good Things" are accessed from the Town Buildings menu (click on the flower). Each item costs the same, and they all increase popularity.

MAYPOLE

Resource Cost	30 Gold
Workers Required	N/A
Buildings Required	N/A
Produces/Allows	Increases Popularity

DANCING BEAR

Resource Cost	30 Gold
Workers Required	N/A
Buildings Required	N/A
Produces/Allows	Increase Popularity

GARDENS (3 TYPES)

Resource Cost	30 Gold
Workers Required	N/A
Buildings Required	N/A
Produces/Allows	Increase Popularity

STATUE

Resource Cost	30 Gold
Workers Required	N/A
Buildings Required	N/A
Produces/Allows	Increase Popularity

SHRINE

Resource Cost	30 Gold
Workers Required	N/A
Buildings Required	N/A
Produces/Allows	Increase Popularity

POND (SMALL OR LARGE)

Resource Cost	30 Gold
Workers Required	N/A
Buildings Required	N/A
Produces/Allows	Increase Popularity

FEAR INDUCERS

Hey, you can't be a nice Lord all the time. When your people are slacking off, throw in a few Fear Inducers to add a spring to their steps. But, don't get carried away. You might increase work efficiency, but your popularity will go into the moat. Select these by clicking the Noose icon on the Town Buildings menu.

GALLOWS

Resource Cost	50 Gold
Workers Required	N/A
Buildings Required	N/A
Produces/Allows	Higher Work Efficiency

CESSPIT

Resource Cost	50 Gold
Workers Required	N/A
Buildings Required	N/A
Produces/Allows	Higher Work Efficiency

STOCKS

Resource Cost	50 Gold
Workers Required	N/A
Buildings Required	N/A
Produces/Allows	Higher Work Efficiency

BURNING STAKE

Resource Cost	50 Gold
Workers Required	N/A
Buildings Required	N/A
Produces/Allows	Higher Work Efficiency

DUNGEON

Resource Cost	50 Gold
Workers Required	N/A
Buildings Required	N/A
Produces/Allows	Higher Work Efficiency

STRETCHING RACK

Resource Cost	50 Gold
Workers Required	N/A
Buildings Required	N/A
Produces/Allows	Higher Work Efficiency

GIBBET

Resource Cost	50 Gold
Workers Required	N/A
Buildings Required	N/A
Produces/Allows	Higher Work Efficiency

CHOPPING BLOCK

Resource Cost	50 Gold
Workers Required	N/A
Buildings Required	N/A
Produces/Allows	Higher Work Efficiency

DUNKING STOOL

Resource Cost	50 Gold
Workers Required	N/A
Buildings Required	N/A
Produces/Allows	Higher Work Efficiency

WEAPONS BUILDINGS

FLETCHER'S WORKSHOP

Resource Cost	20 Wood, 100 Gold
Workers Required	1
Buildings Required	Woodcutter's Hut
Produces/Allows	Bows and Crossbows

The Fletcher is lame, but he still makes a mean bow. You can place Fletcher's Workshops anywhere, but for maximum productivity, position it between the Stockpile and Armory. Don't forget to click on the Bow or Crossbow icon to order your Fletcher to produce the correct weapon for your desired soldier.

POLETURNER'S WORKSHOP

Resource Cost	10 Wood, 100 Gold
Workers Required	1
Buildings Required	Woodcutter's Hut
Produces/Allows	Spears and Pikes

The Poleturner crafts weapons for your Spearmen and Pikemen. Like the Fletcher's Workshop menu, you must select either Spear or Pike to designate a production priority.

BLACKSMITH'S WORKSHOP

Resource Cost	20 Wood, 200 Gold
Workers Required	1
Buildings Required	Iron Mine
Produces/Allows	Maces and Swords

The Blacksmith fashions swords and maces for your Swordsmen, Knights, and Macemen. Like the Fletcher's Workshop menu, you must select either Sword or Mace to produce the desired weapon.

TANNER'S WORKSHOP

Resource Cost	10 Wood, 100 Gold
Workers Required	1
Buildings Required	Dairy Farm
Produces/Allows	Leather Armor

The Tanner designs leather armor for Macemen and Crossbowmen. She slaughters cows for her hides, so she is not a favorite among Dairy Farmers. When you need leather armor, be sure and build several extra Dairy Farms.

ARMORER'S WORKSHOP

Resource Cost	20 Wood, 100 Gold
Workers Required	1
Buildings Required	Iron Mine
Produces/Allows	Metal Armor

The Armorer hammers out suits of armor for Pikemen, Swordsmen, and Knights. You should add extra Iron Mines to meet the Armorer's heavy demands in the advanced Combat missions.

MISCELLANEOUS STRUCTURES

Although you cannot build or alter the following items, they are nonetheless, important to the game. Their significance is explained below.

SIGNPOST

Resource Cost	N/A
Workers Required	N/A
Buildings Required	N/A
Produces/Allows	Marks where Enemy Arrives on the Map

It is a good idea to look for the Signpost before starting your mission. This tells you where to focus your defenses. You should also look for ambush opportunities, where you can slow the enemy advance. This is useful during the first attack, which is usually light. However, we do not recommend this strategy when the enemy charges in with their entire army.

RUINS

Resource Cost	N/A
Workers Required	N/A
Buildings Required	N/A
Produces/Allows	Damaged Stone or Wood can be Replaced
	After the Battle.

Simply place new stone or wood over the damaged section to make it look good as new.

TUNNEL ENTRANCE

Resource Cost	N/A
Workers Required	N/A
Buildings Required	N/A
Produces/Allows	Shows where Tunneler Entered the Ground

When the Tunneler digs in, you'll see the opening. Follow the burrow as it moves toward the enemy tower. The tower will crumble soon after the burrow reaches its destination.

Chapter 5

GENERAL STRATEGIES

This chapter provides you with applied strategies, using all of the fundamental building blocks you've learned about in the previous chapters. Before you can make full use of the information presented here, you should have a comfortable understanding of the buildings and people of the Stronghold world. Every aspect of building, maintaining, expanding, and defending your stronghold is examined here, and with the help of these winning strategies, you'll be able to build legendary fortresses that will stand the test of time and steel.

THE MEDIEVAL ECONOMY

Castles were much more than military fortresses. They stood as a testament to the power of a country's leadership, centers of commerce and government, and homes of the ruling elite. At the heart of every successful stronghold must be a thriving, vibrant economy. You must be able to support your castle's construction with abundant resources, some of which may not be available locally. Those that are not must be traded for, and in turn you must have something to trade. Financial concerns are always central for a Lord, and empty coffers will soon result in an empty castle. This section will help you build a powerful, successful economy capable of supporting all of your needs.

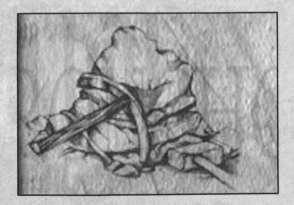

POPULARITY

Popularity is the limiting factor in all economic matters. Ultimately, everything you do outside of warfare is tied to your popularity. Barbaric as it sounds, the only real reason you need to feed your subjects is because they would resent you if you did not. Build too much resentment, and it will lower your Popularity. Once your Popularity falls below 50, your peasants will begin leaving your fiefdom in search of greener pastures. Without peasants, your stronghold will eventually become a ghost town, with no workers, no production, and no future.

Managing your popularity while achieving your goals, therefore, is the main focus of the game. It is so well integrated into gameplay, however, that you won't really notice it, because the Popularity effects are logically and seamlessly blended with the game functions. Naturally, feeding people less results in negative feelings; conversely, paying your subjects a bit of coin each month makes them very happy!

MANAGING MONEY

You need money for the formation of military units, construction of advanced buildings, and purchasing imported goods at the Marketplace. There are two ways to earn money: taxation, and exporting goods. Usually, you'll want to use some combination of the two for the greatest efficiency, but some scenarios will naturally favor one over the other. You should be equally familiar with both methods of earning money so you are able to manage your finances in any situation.

Tip

Although it certainly isn't desirable, bribes (that is, negative tax rates) can help bolster your Popularity in times of emergency. This is yet another reason why you should strive to keep your coffers filled with Gold at all times.

Taxation is set at your keep, where you can select from a wide range of tax levels, from tyranny to a welfare state. Unless things are dramatically wrong with your economy, you don't want to be paying your peasants. Making your peasants pay their taxes causes increasing resentment as the tax rate goes up. Since you'll always seek to tax your peasants in some way, the tax rate is the most common source of negative popularity in your fiefdom.

All other economic factors will usually be making the population happier. This means that the Popularity bonuses from all those other factors (food, Inns, Good Things, religion, etc.) will essentially balance out the unpopularity of taxation. The important thing to do is strike a balance, where your Popularity is holding steady at, or near 100 while you are charging the maximum amount possible in taxes.

The sale of surplus goods in a Marketplace is the second method of earning money in Stronghold. "Surplus" is defined as any resource or manufactured good that is not specifically required for immediate consumption by your own population. Even food, which is *eventually* consumed by your population, can be sold as surplus if you have enough of it. If you are producing more food than your population eats and you have more than a six-month supply in the Granary, you can easily afford to sell the excess. Smaller food reserves will cut it close to the safety margin and restrict your ability to increase your population immediately. Note that some scenarios will only allow you to sell specific types of goods; in these cases, concentrate your industry on producing these saleable goods.

FOOD PRODUCTION

Providing ample food for your peasants is the very first economic priority in Stronghold. At the very least, you must provide one type of food in large enough quantities to support your entire population. Unless you intend to remain stagnant, your food production must outpace your population growth, or you'll find yourself in very uncomfortable times when your population expands (see *Population Growth, below*).

Beyond simply satiating your peasants' hunger, you can actually make them happy (thereby increasing your popularity) by introducing additional types of food to their diet. For each additional food type beyond the first, you'll gain one point of popularity. Each food type must be provided in roughly equal proportion, so one Apple Orchard is not enough to provide a reliable supply of apples for a population of 500. Sometimes, varied food types are available for trade at the Marketplace, in which case it's possible to trade for additional types of food instead of producing them yourself. In this case, you should build additional Granaries to store purchased food stocks, so that you don't have to constantly return to the Market to affect a balanced diet for your serfs.

Tip

Sometimes, war or another kind of emergency will find you with dwindling food stocks and no way to recover before you run out of food. Rather than feed your peasants well until they begin to starve, it's better to extend your food stocks as soon as possible by dropping to half rations, which will buy you time to build more food-producing industry.

You may also increase your Popularity by increasing the amount of food your peasants are allowed to eat. By clicking on the Granary, you can adjust the rations to higher levels, consuming food at an increased rate but also resulting in greater Popularity gains. This can be a very effective way of managing your Popularity, as it requires only manpower to work the extra food industries, and has no side effects.

INDUSTRY

Exploiting natural resources and producing manufactured goods are the keys to building a successful, self-sufficient economy. Industry plays an increasing role in your Stronghold as your population increases, as you build more and larger buildings to support them. The universal resource is wood—you'll need Woodcutters in every single mission that features stronghold building. They should be your first buildings constructed in any scenario, after the required elements (a keep and a Granary) have been placed. If you wait to build your Woodcutters, you may inadvertently run out of wood stocks, which will make any scenario un-winnable.

Beyond wood, you'll probably find stone to be the next most commonly used resource in full-fledged castle building. The walls, towers, gatehouses, and even churches of medieval castles take incredible amounts of quarried stone to build, and it's much cheaper to produce it yourself than to import it from traders at the Market.

Iron and pitch can be gathered for export, or for military purposes. Iron, naturally, is used in the production of weapons, and pitch can be laid into trenches along likely approaches to your castle for burning attacking troops as they advance.

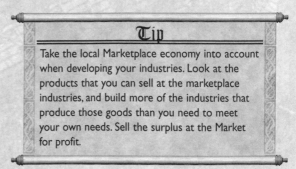

Tip

Take the local Marketplace economy into account when developing your industries. Look at the products that you can sell at the marketplace industries, and build more of the industries that produce those goods than you need to meet your own needs. Sell the surplus at the Market for profit.

Hops Farms and Breweries are also considered industries, as their products are not "food" per se. The population may consume ale at an alarming rate, but it doesn't make them any less hungry—just louder!

RELIGION

No matter what your personal feelings are on spiritual fulfillment, in the Stronghold world religion is nothing more than a method of increasing your Popularity. Each church you build serves to "bless" a certain percentage of your population. The higher your overall percentage of blessed people, the more popular your rule will be. Religion is expensive in terms of building costs and population (some of your peasants will find work in the clergy, which takes them away from more "productive" potential jobs).

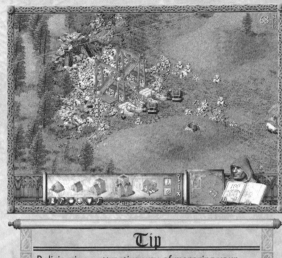

Tip

Religion is an attractive way of managing your Popularity. It takes less labor than the ale industry, and it works without affecting your population's output or effectiveness.

As the size of your population increases, you will receive requests for a larger place of worship. Smaller settlements remain content with a modest Chapel, but sprawling walled cities demand ornate (and expensive) Cathedrals. You must expand your religious coverage along with your population, or you may find yourself suddenly unable to support a tax rate you've grown accustomed to.

BASICS
CHARACTERS
STRUCTURES
GENERAL STRATEGIES
COMBAT MISSIONS
ECONOMIC MISSIONS
MULTIPLAYER
MAPS

BEAUTY AND THE BEAST

A full suite of accoutrements is available for your castle, falling into two broad categories: Good Things, and Bad Things. These two types of buildings and improvements work on opposite ends of the same scale, affecting your castle's Fear Factor. The Fear Factor has a direct effect on the productiveness of your population. With Dungeons, Racks, Stocks, and other Bad Things, you can raise the Fear Factor in your fiefdom, scaring the populace into higher resource output at the cost of a deep plunge in

your Popularity. Alternately, you can choose to beautify your castle with Shrines, Statues, Gardens, and the like, improving your Popularity but lowering the productivity of your subjects as they take long breaks from work to enjoy the lifestyle you've fostered.

Ultimately, choosing to use Good Things or Bad Things is dependent upon the resources available on each map, and the victory conditions of the scenario missions. Increasing production with Bad Things lowers Popularity, which must be compensated with other things: lower taxes, more food, and so on. Both of those things represent a reduction in overall productivity, so the effects balance out somewhat. Conversely, increased Popularity with Good Things lowers production rates, so although you may be able to raise taxes, you'll lose money through the loss of products that could be sold at the Market.

POPULATION GROWTH

Increasing your settlement's population is tricky, and requires a bit of finesse to pull off without causing a food shortage. You should always outpace your population growth with extra food production. Don't rely on building new food industries after you've built another Hovel, because the food production process takes a bit of time (over nine months of game time from wheat seeds to food in the case of the complicated bread industry!), so you will not reap the benefits of new food sources for some time after their establishment. Keep this in mind when planning your growth—have a surplus of food stored up so that the new population doesn't drain your Granary.

MAKING WAR

Unless you are playing one of the Economics scenarios, all things in Stronghold eventually lead to war. Ultimately, a strong economy is not a goal in itself, but a means to and end: you must have a strong economy to support a military force capable of defending your castle. This section will help you create and command a mighty garrison, and provide you with strategies that will grant you victory in battle time and again. You'll also master the art of siege warfare, with sound tactical advice for conducting an attack on an enemy stronghold.

BUILDING A MILITARY FORCE

You begin most scenarios without any military assets. Since you cannot create and fund a military without substantial economic assets, you must first focus on building your economy. Get the wood and food you need to expand your settlement, flowing into your Stockpile and Granary, and tend to your Popularity early on. Recruiting soldiers takes Gold, so you must plan for a way to bring in money, either through taxation or trade. In the latter case, you'll need a Marketplace.

You need a few critical buildings before you can raise an army. First, you must build a Barracks, which houses and trains troops. You must also build an Armory to host your weapon stocks. Lastly, you must either import weapons for your soldiers, or import them at the Marketplace. They are seldom available for import, making manufacture your standard method of acquiring weapons.

Tip

Don't forget to continue expanding your economy as you build up your military infrastructure. Letting your economy stagnate while you focus on military buildup will lead to disaster in the long run, as later expansion will be severely dampened.

Weapons production requires iron and wood, so you must build an extra Woodcutter and one or more Iron Mines. You may alternately import Iron, if it is available for trade. All this trading can get very expensive, which again illustrates the need for a healthy economy and ample tax or trade revenues to support your military. Recruitment itself also costs Gold!

When you have all the pieces in place and you've begun filling your Armory with weapons, you may begin recruiting soldiers. Each soldier comes from your population of unemployed peasants, which is yet another strain on your economy. People working as soldiers still consume food, but contribute absolutely nothing to your production economy. A working bread industry is absolutely essential for the support of a military of any substantial size, as it is the only way for a few hands to feed many more times their number. You should still try to provide varied food types, to boost your Popularity and allow you to levy higher taxes to support your troops.

Engineers are a special troop type, and they are essential to the fully prepared castle defense. Instead of training at a Barracks, these highly skilled professionals are created at an Engineer's Guild, where they study to learn the art of medieval combat engineering. They do not require any weapons to produce, making them attractive early units so that you have *someone* manning the ramparts in case of enemy attack. However, they are no good on their own. Engineers can either be turned into Laddermen (to assist you in scaling enemy walls), or they can be assigned to man a war engine. The latter job is the only one applicable to castle defense, so this is how you'll usually employ them.

You may build war engines like Ballistas or Mangonels, at a high price in gold. Place them atop your towers to provide your castle with ample firepower to employ against any attackers. Enemy siege engines are among the greatest threats to your castle, and a well-placed Ballista can help you destroy them before they have a chance to knock down your walls. Mangonels may also be used against enemy troops, and are particularly effective against massed approaching infantry.

Both of these engines are nothing more than large mechanical curiosities until you assign two Engineers to man them. Select two Engineers by clicking and dragging around them, and then click on the engine you wish them to crew. As soon as they take their positions beside the machine, it is ready to fire.

The best military force is a balanced one. No one type of troop can win a battle on its own; it takes a combination of many different troop types to truly excel on the battlefield. On the defense, your primary unit should be Archers. You should have some melee troops (Spearmen or Macemen) to push ladders off your walls and defend against potential breaches. You should also have some war engines manned by Engineers to provide counter-fire against enemy siege engines, which can dish out horrendous amounts of punishment to your walls. By building a balanced force capable of responding to any potential threat, you will be able to defend your castle successfully against enemy armies many times larger than your garrison.

DEFENDING YOUR CASTLE

Since Stronghold is about building and defending a castle, you'll usually find yourself cast in the role of defender. As such, you must master the art of defense to preserve your people, and the hard work you have invested in building your stronghold.

Defense in depth is one of the most important concepts of castle defense. Unless you have been placed in charge of a castle that has already been constructed with a single wall, you should always endeavor to have more than one line of defense. An inner wall surrounding your keep and essential buildings will allow your troops to fall back from the outer wall if an enemy overwhelms the outer ring of defenses. Enemy siege engines can make short work of walls, making a second line of defense very important. As the enemy soldiers trickle through the gaps they have created in the outer wall, melee soldiers stationed in the outer bailey can gang up on them while Archers atop the inner wall lend fire support.

Tip

Station as many defenders as you can in towers, which are much more resistant to enemy attack than walls. They are also taller, which provides your Archers with greater range and offensive bonuses when firing.

You should spread out your defenders along the wall (or walls) facing the enemy attack, so that you are firing on them from as many sides as possible. The attacker can use Portable Shields to protect advancing troops from missile fire in one direction, but as they near your walls, towers to either side of them will begin firing from both sides of the attackers, making the protection offered by the Portable Shields inadequate. Corner towers are especially important, as they can also fire down the sides of the castle in case the enemy runs the gauntlet of fire and attempts an attack on the flank.

THE ART OF SIEGE WARFARE

Attacking an enemy stronghold is a great challenge, and it requires careful planning and precise execution. Remember that the defender has almost all the advantages of terrain and position, so you have to overcome those advantages with sound tactics, superior numbers, and determination.

The first consideration of any attack must be the enemy walls, as you must get past them in order to achieve victory. Have a clear plan for overcoming the enemy wall. You may choose to scale them, knock them down, or go through the Gatehouse. Each approach has its own advantages and disadvantages, and you must consider each scenario independently to decide which is the most suitable approach.

UP AND OVER

If the enemy walls are simply too strong for you to pick through, tunnel under, knock down with siege engines, or otherwise breach, climbing over them where they stand may be your only chance for entry into the castle. Scaling the walls requires Laddermen and melee troops. You may also move Siege Towers up to the walls, if you have the resources available.

Enemy troops atop the ramparts will be able to push your ladders off the wall, so it is important to support them with Archers and/or Crossbowmen. Target enemy troops atop the walls to keep their heads down while your infantry bravely rushes up the ladders; or better yet, use your Archers to eliminate the wall garrison before placing your ladders. Inevitably, your troops will be exposed to the full force of the enemy Archers atop the defending towers, so you can expect heavy casualties in a ladder assault. If you have Engineers available, build Portable Shields to help protect your army as it advances on the wall.

BREACHING THE WALLS

If you can muster the firepower, knocking down the enemy walls is the best, safest choice for the attack. Fire boulders from your siege engines from a great distance away, out of range of defending Archers. Unless the enemy has war engines of their own atop the defending towers, you can continue your bombardment with impunity. Tunnelers can also undermine walls, and can be very effective over the course of an extended siege. Even melee troops (especially Macemen) can use picks to grind through the walls, though this method should only be used as a last resort, and only if the enemy has very few Archers covering the outer wall.

Work towards creating a breach in the walls large enough to accommodate the bulk of your army, so that they can flood through the hole in one large group. If the breach is too small, only a few of your troops will be able to enter the castle at one time, allowing the enemy to fight at even odds against your soldiers as they gain the outer bailey.

If the enemy still isn't responding to your attack, move your siege engines up, and attempt to destroy the next line of walls. Your siege engines are nearly useless after you've entered the castle, so once they have developed a breach in the outer wall you may employ them more recklessly. If they are drawing enemy fire, move your Archers forward to return fire and give the enemy additional targets. Once your siege engines are destroyed or ineffective, rush forward with your entire army.

Tip

If possible, try to preserve the outer towers. You can station your own troops atop them once the hand-to-hand battle has swept past them, granting you some of the same advantages formerly held exclusively by the defenders.

THE GATEHOUSE

Although often overlooked, the Gatehouse is often the best point of attack. Wooden Gatehouses are particularly vulnerable to attack by Battering Rams, so you should evaluate the strength of the

Tip

Take care in the placement of your Siege Tents, which will eventually become your siege engines. Mobile siege engines, like Battering Rams and Siege Towers, should be placed out of range of the enemy Archers. Move them forward, only when you can they can reach the wall intact. It only takes a single hit from a Ballista, or a hail of arrows from Crossbowmen to shatter a siege engine.

enemy Gatehouse as you plan your attack. Sometimes, a castle's Gatehouse will be under built, making it the weakest point in the outer wall. Depending on a castle's design, a Gatehouse may also be the key to the entire castle. If the enemy castle isn't designed well, a breach at the Gatehouse could open the entire bailey to an invading army.

If you choose to attack the gatehouse, concentrate all of your efforts against it. Blow through the doors with a Battering Ram, demolish the entire structure with Trebuchets and Catapults, or overwhelm it with infantry. Once you've gained entry, flood the gap with everything you have.

FINISHING THE ATTACK

Once you've broken through the walls, concentrate all of your efforts on reaching the enemy keep and defeating the Lord of the castle. Do not worry about hunting down the rest of the enemy garrison, as they will surrender as soon as their commander has fallen. It takes several regular infantrymen to defeat the Lord, who is quite good in hand-to-hand combat. You will have better luck with Swordsmen

> ### Tip
> Be wary of troops hiding inside the keep. Some enemy guards may be hidden from view until you attack. If you suspect strong resistance, send the first squad into the building and see if they arrive at the top of the keep intact. If you hear fighting inside the keep, and your squad does not return, reinforce your next squad with heavy infantry (Macemen and Swordsmen) and try it again.

or Macemen, but even a squad of Spearmen will be able to take him down together. Move to surround him before you attack, so that all of your troops are hitting him at the same time. When the Lord falls, the castle - and victory - are yours!

CASTLE DESIGN

Designing a castle requires a harmony of economic and military concerns. A successful castle must be able to function both as a formidable defensive stronghold and a viable economic center. If it fails in the former regard, all your building will be for naught, as your castle will fall to the first enemy that comes along with a force powerful enough to defeat your inadequate defenses. Fail in the latter, and once again your castle will fall, this time to the burden of its own economic weight. Both goals must be considered in harmony in order to construct an ideal castle.

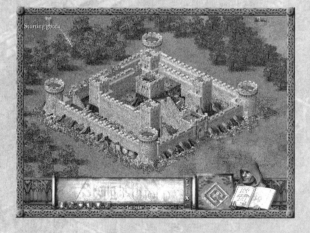

LINES OF DEFENSE

Think of the military plan of your castle before you build a single structure. Look for the sign-post on the map, which marks the invasion point for enemy armies. The side of your castle that faces that point will bear the brunt of all enemy attacks. Work out a plan to provide your troops with concentric rings of walls to allow them to execute a successful defense in depth, with strong fallback positions to serve them even if the outer wall is taken. If you need to, you can even sketch out a plan on a piece of paper.

Tip

Study the histories of the castles described in the Siege missions, and pay attention to the plans of the ones that were most successful in battle. Learn from their designs, and try to incorporate the most successful elements of those castles in your plans.

Your plan must take the natural terrain into account, and it should include economic considerations. Is there a natural defensive position? Where is the most fertile ground? Where will you get stone for your walls, wood for your buildings, and iron for your weapons? How will workers flow in and out of the castle on the way to those buildings? If you build a castle with gates that are too convoluted, your workers will waste much of their time walking the maze to get in and out of the castle to deposit goods in your Stockpile. Provide your people with good traffic flow while maintaining your castle's security.

ECONOMIC CONSIDERATIONS

Once you have the overall position and plan of your castle in mind, you must modify it to accommodate your industry. A castle must make very efficient use of the space within its walls, devoting every square inch of space to critical buildings. Anything outside of your walls faces the possibility of demolition at the hands of an invading army; so keep as much as you can within the safety of your defenses. Conversely, it doesn't make military sense to spread your defenses out all over the map, so some buildings will have to run the risk of being overrun in the event of war.

Farms, Woodcutters, Hunter's Posts, and other inexpensive buildings are logical choices for buildings placed outside your defensive perimeter. These are relatively inexpensive to replace, and either take up a large amount of space, or require specific conditions for placement. While a river valley is a prime location for an Apple Orchard, it is not necessarily the best place to fight a war.

Out of Sight, Out of Mind

If an unprotected Dairy Farm lies in the path of advancing infantry, chances are the animals and caretakers will be slaughtered. However, if the same farm is even partially hidden by a wall, the soldiers may continue toward the castle walls, ignoring the civilians. Consider shielding, or even completely enclosing your exposed work sites. There is one caveat: the new enclosures may alter the defensive sight lines on your original walls, so might need to make adjustments so the new wall is covered.

You should provide at least a moderate capacity to produce food within your castle, so that you will be less susceptible to starvation from a long siege. Your bread industry, which is expensive and cumbersome, is an excellent candidate for inclusion inside your castle walls. Wheat Farms are the smallest farms in the game, and should be located close to your Stockpile. With even one Mill and accompanying set of Wheat Farms and Bakeries, you can produce enough food to weather an extended siege.

DEFENDING YOUR ASSETS

All of your military buildings should be in or near the innermost ring of your castle's defenses, to provide them with the greatest amount of protection from enemy attack as possible. If you were to lose your ability to make new troops in between battles, you could be doomed by the next attack. Protect your Armory especially, which hosts all of your expensive weapons.

Naturally, your keep should be within your very innermost ring of defenses. Since it cannot be closed to the enemy, you must construct an inner castle to defend it, complete with one or more Gatehouses and ample towers to provide for the defense. Your keep should be located on the single most defensible spot in your stronghold. Feel free to employ dirty tricks around its walls, including Oil Smelters, Killing Pits, Pitch Ditches, or anything else you think will aid in the final defense.

Tip

Pitch Ditches are best used in long, slender trenches along the enemy's most likely line of advance. Tend towards several smaller ditches instead of fewer large ones, so that you can set fire to specific patches of ground without wasting pitch on empty ground. Build several rows of trenches, as well, to get multiple burns along the same route.

Lay out your buildings with your castle walls in mind even before you begin building them. It is a waste of resources and time to destroy and rebuild misplaced buildings, so try to build in straight lines, without any wasted space between buildings. Remember, your peasants also need space to walk between buildings, so leave one to two space passages in between your structures, and make sure they follow the logical flow of traffic. If you plan on having large stocks of food and goods, you should also plan for the eventual expansion of your Granary and Stockpile. Since these can only be placed adjacent to their existing partners, you must leave room for them that won't disrupt traffic flow.

If you anticipate early attacks, get a wooden palisade up around your inner keep. It's important to have at least something in place to defend your citizens, and you can always replace the wooden stockade with stone later. With a grand design in mind and your industry growing according to the planned layout of your walls, you are ready to work towards the distant goal of building a stronghold that will stand the test of time and war.

Chapter 6

COMBAT CAMPAIGN

1 GATHERING THE LOST

Objectives

Acquire Food: 20 Meat

Acquire Goods: 40 Wood

We need you to oversee the setting up of a good-sized base camp. Start by finding a suitable clearing then use some of the wood plentiful in this area to begin the construction.

The first order of business is to place a Keep and Granary. This mission ends so quickly; there's no need to spend time mulling over the perfect locations. A Hunter brings a dressed kill back to the Granary from wherever he happens to take down an animal. When building a castle, this location takes on new importance. However, for now, just drop the Granary anywhere in the vicinity.

There are no demands to build anything here, or to conserve any original resources, so feel free to place three Woodcutter's Huts adjacent to the closest forest. Two Hunter's Posts are sufficient, because unlike the trees, a wild herd moves after every kill, so there is no real advantage to placing multiple huts in the same area. However, it's possible to "herd" the herd, by placing two Hunter's Posts, one on either side of the map. There is a good chance the herd will run in the other direction after the first Hunter bags a kill.

Within moments, you receive word that wolves are on the prowl, but don't worry. The Stockpile and Granary fill quickly, taking you to the first campaign victory. The wolves are not a factor…at least not yet.

2 FINISHING THE FORT

Objectives

Acquire Food: 35 Meat

Complete Castle

To ensure the safety of the men, you are required to renovate the abandoned stockade before winter is upon us again. Use the archers to kill off any wolves that threaten the peasants.

At the beginning of the mission, three groups of wolves lounge in the forest along the northern edge of the map. What this means is you must weather three separate attacks while building out the stockade and accumulating 35 units of meat. Fortunately, four trained Archers are hanging around the platform above the gate. From this vantage point, they can easily pick-off the wolves before they reach the gate. Direct all Archers to take an "Aggressive" stance, so they will respond quickly to the attacking wolves.

Now that the protection is set, build one Woodcutter's Hut just outside the unfinished wall. There's enough wood in the opening Stockpile to enclose most of the stockade, so one hut is plenty. Finally, place four Hunter's Posts in front of the gate. Keeping them close to the Gatehouse allows the Archers to protect the Hunters while they are preparing their meat.

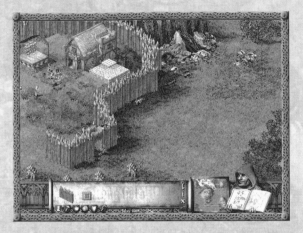

All of the wolf attacks come from the north. The animals creep along the wall, trying to stay out of sight until they reach the compound. However, the elevated Archers take care of most of the wolves before they reach the gate. Two of the three wolf packs attack first, and they are ferocious. The hunters and woodcutters will join in the defense, but they are not as adept as the Archers are, so don't depend on them to do the job.

Keep an eye on the Stockpile and build out the stockade when wood becomes available. The Archers should take care of the wolves, allowing the Hunters to fill the Granary. When you reach 35 Meat (and the stockade is fully enclosed), claim the second victory!

3 ELIMINATING THE WOLVES

Objectives

Eradicate Wolves
Construct a Motte and bailey fortification and strengthen it with some towers. Then start bow production and raise a force of archers with which to eradicate the wolves that run riot there.

Winning this mission is all about killing wolves. Although the objectives also include the construction of a fortified Motte and bailey, it's not required to achieve victory. However, if you build a wall around the Keep and add at least one Gate, it will be easier to protect the Peasants, who are needed for Archer training. Place the Keep on the raised clearing east of the river. You need a substantial amount of wood to build a Barracks, Armory, and Fletcher's Workshop (for bow production and Archer training), so we recommend two Woodcutter's Huts just east of the river. The wolves do not attack early in the mission, so concentrate on accumulating wood, and constructing the aforementioned buildings. Eventually, you'll need to raise taxes to fill the treasury, because it costs 12 pieces of gold to train an Archer. The Peasants are not crazy about high taxes, so try to keep them well fed. A Peasant who is broke and hungry is likely to leave the castle. One Hunter's Post is sufficient to keep everyone in ham hocks.

After bow production is up and running, add a Gate at the rear of the outpost. As the Archers are trained, position at least two (three is even better) on the platform overlooking the front Gate (closest to the river) and two more at the back Gate. The Archers closest to the river will kill most of the wolves, while those stationed at the rear will take care of de Puce's men (more on them later). Raise the taxes as needed, to train Archers, and lower them as soon as possible. If the taxes remain high for too long, the Peasants will split. If this happens, simply bribe them until they come back, and then immediately train them as Archers.

Tip

If a wolf attack goes bad and eliminates the remaining Peasants, put the Woodcutters to sleep (they will become Peasants), and then immediately train them as Archers.

If the defenses fail and the wolves get inside the gate, the Lord of the Keep can single-handedly defeat ten wolves or more. However, this is an emergency tactic, and not a recommended strategy. Remember that the mission is over when the character dies; so don't get too aggressive with the big guy.

As we mentioned earlier, de Puce's scouts arrive from the east, and you receive a warning that they will send word of the position back to their castle. Don't worry, the Archers will dispose of them in short order, and despite the warning, they cannot keep you from earning a victory. Just stay focused on the wolves, because you must kill them all to win the mission.

4 THE HIDDEN LOOKOUT

Objectives

Eliminate All Enemy Units

Find a suitable location on high ground near the lands belonging to Duc de Puce and start construction of an outpost. The wooden keep will offer better protection than a simple hall. Take some cattle to breed as the land there suits them well. Do not show thyself to the enemy, but should you be discovered, let none escape to tell. The hills will give the archers an advantage when firing from height.

The strategy for this mission can be distilled into a simple sentence, "Get thee to high ground!" because without elevated platforms for the Archers, the Duke's army will cut you to pieces. The action picks up quickly in this mission, so get busy building an outpost. Place the Keep in the center of the map in the middle of a large, barren plateau. Immediately construct a wall running south to the edge of the map. This will deplete the wood stores rather quickly, so build at least two Woodcutter's Huts to replenish the supply. There is enough forest within the compound, so build them to the west of the new wall.

Begin construction of the second wall running northwest from the point of the first wall. After placing five or six timbers, add a Gate to the new wall (it should face northeast), and then continue the wall as far as possible toward the northwest corner of the map. Now, concentrate on training Archers, which requires a Barracks, an Armory, and a Fletcher's Workshop. The first attack is imminent, but it is relatively light. If you can get at least three Archers to the Gate platform, you should survive without losing any Peasants.

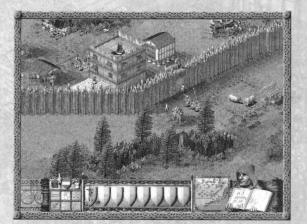

With the walls completed, concentrate on training Archers. However, you must also think about food, because by now, the Granary stores will be depleted. Build a Hunter's Post inside the outpost, and a Dairy Farm on the grassy pasture just outside the gate. This farm is the only structure placed outside the safety of the walls. However, if you build it close to the main gate, the Archers will be able to protect the workers (at least during the early part of the mission) and keep a steady stream of milk and cheese flowing into the Granary. You might want to consider enclosing the Dairy Farm if the Rat's soldiers make a habit of destroying it.

As the army of Archers grows, fill the platform above the gate, and place a few more atop the Keep. The walls should keep the attackers from entering the outpost, but even if they do, the Archers on the Keep will end their miserable lives before they can inflict any real damage. Now, it's just a matter of time. When the Archers kill the last of De Puce's soldiers, victory is yours!

5 BETWEEN A ROCK AND A HARD PLACE

Objectives

Eliminate All Enemy Units

The scouts report that you're trapped without enough supplies to continue or enough troops to fight the way back. The only chance is to make the stand here. They have found a strong defensive position on an island in a broad river and one of the lieutenants has already started building a base. The land around the river is very fertile; use it to grow some wheat.

They say no man is an island, but in this case, neither is the kingdom. You are trapped on an island that is large enough to hold a castle, but resources are severely limited. The first order of business is to cut off access to the island by building five Gatehouses, each one blocking a river ford (look for stepping stones in the water). Place four Woodcutter's Huts immediately, and continue building fortifications as wood becomes available. If you can build the north and east Gatehouses before the first attack, you will be able to repel the enemy with just the four original Archers.

The next attack is considerably stronger, so work quickly. Finish the fortifications at the river fords, but don't forget about food production. Build a Wheat Farm, and then add a Windmill (for flour) and a Bakery. A couple of Hunter's Posts will help keep the Granary packed to the rafters. You'll need plenty of food stores to dole out Double Rations. This is the best way to entice the Peasants to pay higher taxes, which in turn, supports the cost of training Archers. Remember, a Fletcher's Workshop costs 100 pieces of gold, so you need to inspire the loyal subjects to dig deep and support a strong military. Don't forget a Barracks and Armory to round out the Archer training cycle.

Double-rations keep the Peasants plump and happy, and they reward you by filling the treasury at a brisk pace. Keep close tabs on the Barracks, and pump out Archers as fast as possible. If you can afford it, add another Fletcher's Workshop to speed up Bow production. You'll need about a dozen Archers to fend off the second attack.

Now for the grand finale. The Rat pulls out his siege engines in the final battle so don't be surprised to see the walls come tumbling down when the Catapults start firing. It's a good idea to shore up the Gatehouses with extra rows of timbers to give them a little more staying power. If a Gatehouse crumbles under the attack, send the displaced Archers to the top of the Keep. The battle is fast and furious, but if you have enough bows firing, you'll outlast the Rat and claim another victory for the good guys.

6 THE RAT'S PROPOSAL

Objectives

Negotiate With the Rat

From Lord Woolsack: Pitch a small camp in an open clearing then await Duc de Puce's arrival. Do not bring arms to bear upon him for any reason. To secure our lands these talks must succeed.

Surprise! The diplomatic party was ambushed and destroyed. Now it's time for the real mission.

Objectives

Eliminate All Enemy Units

From Sir Longarm: A trap. Our advance party was mown down like animals. Now I will give you some new orders. Build a large fortification and prepare the troops for Duc de Puce's arrival. Use the masons I sent with you to quarry stone and build a strong and permanent castle here.

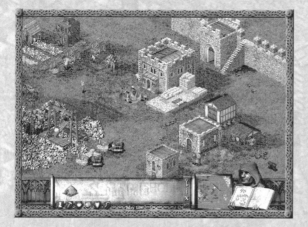

After placing the Keep and Granary near the stone deposit, build a Quarry, Ox Tether, and extra Stockpile (the original one fills almost instantly). Although the castle will be stone, you need wood for weapons production, so we recommend two Woodcutter's Huts (a thick forest lies northwest of the Keep). Add a Hunter's Post and Wheat Farm for food production, and don't forget to add a Windmill and Bakery when wood supply allows. Finally, a Barracks, Armory, and Fletcher's Workshop round out the core buildings. Keep close tabs on weapon production and trains Archers as quickly as possible.

Warning

Large, nasty, bears frequent the castle, and they must be killed, or you lose valuable workers. Hunters target them automatically, but they cannot defend themselves from close range attacks. The threat is greatly reduced after you train several Archers and place them atop the Gatehouses where they can control the bear population.

Unlike the previous mission, the Rat comes in hard on his first attack. Archers lead the way, but it is the Catapult that does serious damage from its hidden position behind a large rock outcropping. You'll need a Gatehouse, a Crenellated Wall, and at least eight Archers to weather the initial attack. Spread the Archers along the wall where they can target enemy Spearmen who breach the wall. Take care not to expose the Lord of the castle to enemy attackers, unless it is a one-on-one fight.

After the battle, repair the walls immediately, and go back to producing Archers. Another attack is imminent, but this time, you can be better prepared. First, build a second wall in front of the existing wall. It doesn't stop the attack, but it slows down the enemy, and more importantly, it absorbs the Catapult barrage. When the enemy soldiers finally approach the castle, they are greatly depleted, and make easy targets for the Archers.

While awaiting the third attack, rebuild the exterior wall, and use any extra stone to extend the interior wall of the castle. By now, you should have 12-15 Archers, and you'll need every one of them to survive the final battle. Keep expanding the force, and spread out the Archers along the walls. The Rat gives it one more try, with more of the same: Catapults, Archers and Spearmen. Once again, they focus on destroying the exterior wall, giving the Archers excellent field of vision to target the foot soldiers as they walk around the wall. It's a bloodbath for the Rat, but it couldn't happen to a nicer guy.

7 BREAKING THE SIEGE

BASICS

CHARACTERS

STRUCTURES

GENERAL STRATEGIES

COMBAT MISSIONS

ECONOMIC MISSIONS

MULTIPLAYER

MAPS

Objectives

Eliminate All Enemy Units

Lord Manikin is under siege and it is vital to our cause that his county does not fall. Land by boat with a company of spearmen and command his garrison to victory. Success here may well spark uprisings from some of the other counties.

In the previous mission, it took a second stone wall to keep the enemy Catapults from destroying the castle. This was a critical strategy, because despite the Archers, it was impossible to destroy the enemy siege equipment. Now, there's a new weapon: Spearmen. These warriors can protect Archers from close range attacks, and they can destroy siege equipment.

However, as this mission begins, there's little time for strategy. The Rat's troops attack immediately after the start of the mission, sending Archers, waves of Spearmen, and ladder carriers. There are only three Archers deployed on wooden towers in front of the castle, hardly a strong enough force to stop the invasion. Withdraw the Archers to the Gatehouse, and call up the 20 Spearmen and six Archers who are lounging on the beach in the southeast corner of the map. Send the Spearmen to the stone wall where they push the ladders down. Keep targeting the enemy Archers until they are eliminated, and then send the Spearmen to destroy the Siege Equipment.

After the first siege is over, repair the stone walls, reinforcing them with Crenellated sections. Instead of rebuilding the outer wooden wall, erect a stone wall behind the remains. Another attack is coming, but now you have time to prepare. Spread out the Spearmen along the castle wall where they will be able to quickly push down the enemy ladders. The Rat sends more Archers this time; so don't forget to keep training Archers of the own. There is new siege equipment, but don't be overanxious. Stay on the walls and methodically eliminate the enemy Archers.

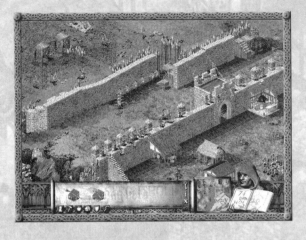

Warning

Don't forget to pull the Spearmen off the wall after they dispose of the ladder carriers. If they stay on the wall, the enemy Archers will pick them off.

Just like in the previous mission, the second wall forces the advancing Spearmen to walk around in orderly fashion, presenting perfect targets for the elevated Archers. Keep firing until the remaining enemy troops retreat.

Now, it's rebuilding time again, in preparation for the final siege. Strengthen the walls and re-deploy the Spearmen and Archers on the wall. Once again, the key is keeping the exterior wall strong. The attacking soldiers must take time to knock down, climb over, or move around this wall, giving the Archers time to mow them down. When the enemy forces dwindle to a handful of Archers and Spearmen, the Rat calls a retreat. If you like order in the castle, rebuild the damaged walls. But, it isn't necessary, because in a few minutes you'll hear the Rat's whiny voice lamenting the latest victory.

BASICS

CHARACTERS

STRUCTURES

GENERAL STRATEGIES

COMBAT MISSIONS

ECONOMIC MISSIONS

MULTIPLAYER

MAPS

8 DEALING WITH THE DEVIL

Objectives

Acquire Goods: 10 Ale

Eliminate All Enemy Units

Spies report that the Rat is due to launch a do or die attack on our lands and you must intercept and delay his forces. There is no time to raise an army but Duc Beauregard (the Snake) will send a large force to help us in return for a shipment of ale. Once the Rat's siege force is defeated, Beauregard has agreed to let us take the Rat's neighboring county without resistance. Grow hops and brew ale to send to the Snake but be warned, it will be hard to keep the people in line whilst meeting the terms of the deal. Use any means at the disposal, even cruelty if necessary, the Rat's force must be defeated here.

As the mission begins, the challenge is to accumulate 10 kegs of ale to send to the Snake. In return, he will dispatch reinforcements to help you fend off the Rat's impending attack. Sounds reasonable, but the problem is, you must also defend the settlement against several smaller attacks until help arrives. This presents two challenges that require the immediate attention: develop an ale industry, and protect the settlement. Doing both at the same time requires considerable resources and a large force of workers and soldiers.

The only fertile ground on the map lies in a narrow valley east of the rock deposit. Not only is this area a considerable trek from the keep, it is a nightmare to defend. Nevertheless, you must quickly build a Hops Farm, which produces the main ingredient for making ale. When you place the Hops Farm, choose a location that leaves the shortest distance to the Stockpile, because hops have a tendency to rot if they are left on the vines too long.

Also, keep in mind that a Wheat Farm is the only food producing option in this mission. Like hops, wheat must be harvested quickly, so keep a clear path to the Stockpile. We recommend placing one on each side of the fertile land. This will save room for the Quarry, and allow you to place additional farms later.

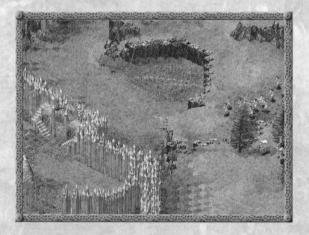

The Rat attacks the settlement soon after you begin the mission. Of course, they will target the hops and wheat farmers, so you must provide protection. We recommend a timber wall and Gatehouse protecting the farms, and stretching back toward the keep. Bring up three Spearmen to provide backup if the Rat's soldiers break through the wall. These attacks continue, so you must fall into a routine of reinforcing the troops and strengthening the walls between battles. After the first attack, there should be enough stone to upgrade the walls and add a stone Gatehouse.

The plot thickens when the Snake sends a message, requesting double the amount of ale (20 kegs). There's no choice but to comply because without his reinforcements, there's no chance against the Rat's final siege. Add a second Hops Farm and two more Breweries. Although it's possible to raise the popularity by building an Inn, it's best not to deplete the ale stock until you satisfy the Snake's requirement. Instead, build a few "good buildings" like Gardens, Monuments, or Maypoles (for the kiddies).

With the ale industry cranking at full capacity, concentrate on feeding the population and building the military. Balance the tax rate to bring in enough gold for weapons, but don't let it get high enough to inspire an exodus of Peasants. After shipping the Snake's ale, the reinforcements arrive. But, don't get too complacent. The final attack is massive, including Catapults that will make mincemeat of the carefully reinforced stone walls. You need a split force of Archers that can simultaneously rain arrows on the advancing Spearmen and enemy Archers. The Rat's Archers take up position off to the side, while the Spearmen charge right for the gate (or the hole where it used to be!). Keep a large force of Spearmen behind the walls. You'll need them to defeat the attackers, and then advance into the forest and destroy the siege equipment. When the last Rat man is down, victory is yours!

⑨ THE RAT'S LAST STAND

Objectives

Eliminate All Enemy Units

Defend the Rat's castle against its former owner! It is very badly designed so you will need to strengthen it. Time spent finishing his moat would be well spent. This is an excellent opportunity to finish off one of the Tyrants for good.

This defensive mission introduces moat building, and the availability of stone towers. The Rat's attack is imminent, and you must get to work quickly, strengthening both the castle and the military force. The first job is to direct three Spearmen to finish the Moat on the west side of the castle. Simply point them to the ground adjacent to the castle, and they will whip out their shovels. The attack comes from the south, so you need to strengthen the defenses around the gate. Place Perimeter Turrets on either corner, surrounding the Drawbridge, and a third turret at the northwest corner. Archers in the latter location can target enemy Spearmen as they fill in the Moat.

Reinforced by the Pig, the Rat's attack force is loaded with Spearmen; so don't even think about venturing out of the castle. The most lethal weapons are the Archers who can pick off attackers from their elevated positions. However, the enemy Catapults make short work of the walls, so be sure and move the Archers to the turrets or Gatehouse before the battle begins.

After the first battle, direct all the energies to rebuilding the damaged walls, Moat, and Perimeter Turret. For Moat repairs, you must first go to the Gatehouse menu, and select the Dig Moat icon. Then, click and drag the cursor across the area that requires filling. Direct the Spearmen to the area and they will remove the mud left by the previous attackers. Don't hesitate to widen the Moat; it will take that much longer for the Rat's attackers to fill it in.

Tip

If the Catapults destroy the Perimeter Turret, move the surviving Archers back into the castle. Keep firing at the enemy soldiers as they fill in the Moat. Finally, send the Spearmen to the opening. By the time the enemy Spearmen fill in the moat their forces will be somewhat depleted. Move in quickly with the Spearmen and eliminate the attackers.

Now, concentrate on managing the economy, popularity, and productivity. The second attack makes the first one look like a high school dance, so this is the only time to build a substantial army. You will need 25-30 Archers and 15-20 Spearmen to survive the onslaught; maximize weapons production while attracting more Peasants to the castle with bribes, "good buildings" and plenty of food. Fortunately, the treasury is fat at the beginning of this mission, and you will need every piece of gold to build a strong defense force.

When the attack begins, keep the Archers on high ground (this can be a challenge when the walls and turrets come tumbling down). Winning this final battle requires you to micro-manage each Archer, keeping a steady flow of arrows directed toward the advancing Spearmen, and the Archers who are firing from across the Moat. Move several Spearmen to the top of the keep, where they can protect the Lord. It is likely a few enemy Spearmen will reach the top of the keep, and the Lord's "bodyguards" will even the score. The castle will look like a pile of rubble as the battle reaches its peak, but don't despair. Keep firing, and above all, keep the enemy Spearmen away from the Lord. The last man standing wins!

10 THE SNAKE HUNT BEGINS

Objectives

Achieve Population: 50

Blessed %: 75

The Snake's men are halfway through building a castle in the next county. Chase out the few guards he has placed there, and then finish the construction yourself. The Snake will undoubtedly try to retake the castle, so defend it well.

As the mission begins, you command a force of 30 Spearmen and 10 Archers. The Snake's unfinished castle lies to the north, and it is protected by a handful of Archers and Macemen. Two Archers are waiting in the first turret, and the remaining soldiers are atop the keep. If you take an aggressive approach, you can storm the keep, easily killing the soldiers. However, you will suffer a few casualties along the way. Instead, send a few Spearmen up to the first turret to take out the Archers, while at the same time, sending Archers up to the vacated second turret. When they arrive, order the Archers to lob arrows at the top of the keep, while sending the remaining Spearmen into the keep from the ground. It will all be over in a matter of seconds, and the casualties will be kept to a minimum.

Warning

Don't be fooled by how easily you dispose of the Macemen. They arrive in greater numbers later in the mission, and run through the Spearmen with ease.

Although rabbits and wolves are not as dangerous as enemy soldiers, they are nonetheless troublesome in this mission. It's a good idea to post a few Archers near the Quarry and Wheat Farms. Wolves like to eat Peasants, and rabbits can turn a Wheat Farm into crumbs in record time. Occasionally, the wolves eat the rabbits, saving you a few arrows. But, don't depend on their efforts, because they would just as soon eat a farmer as a bunny. A little advance planning will preserve the valuable resources.

As we mentioned earlier, the Snake's Macemen are big and powerful, and their numbers increase with each attack. However, they are still susceptible to Archers. If you want to withstand the Snake's repeated assaults, build three Fletcher's Workshops and churn out three or four Archers to every Spearman. Position the Archers in the turrets and Gatehouse, and rain arrows down on the advancing Macemen as soon as they come within range.

Archers alone are not enough to stop the Snake's army. You need to construct a stone wall to seal off the entire valley. Add a Gatehouse, and keep training Archers to man the walls. Aside from slowing down the enemy Macemen, the wall also protects the vital farms and Quarry. You need a steady supply of stone from the Quarry to repair the walls between attacks. And, of course, the farms must produce a steady stream of food if you are going to boost the population to 50.

After you establish a strong defense, focus on improving the quality of life within the castle. Keep taxes at a reasonable level, monitor the food supply, and periodically add Hovels to accommodate the growing population. As for the religious objective, you'll need at least three Chapels to achieve 75% coverage. The priests "bless" people as they walk around the castle, and due to the size of the settlement, you'll need at least three Chapels to cover the upper and lower areas of the map.

11 FIRST BLOOD

Objectives

Eliminate All Enemy Units

Advance into the next of the Snake's counties and defend yourself against his forces. This county shares its borders with the Wolf, so stay alert, as you will need to react quickly if he decides to show his face.

This mission introduces the Wolf, whose counties border the Snake's. More importantly, this is your first experience with Swordsmen. A Swordsman's metal armor makes him impervious to arrows, so regular Archers are ineffective. Fortunately, you can train Macemen in this mission, but they are still unable to defeat a Swordsman one-on-one. The key to defeating the Wolf is the ability to manufacture crossbows, and this process is secretly revealed by the hooded stranger midway through the mission.

First things first; let's place the keep. Although there are better strategic locations on this large map, build the keep along the southern border, close to the rock deposit. Here, there's fertile land for planting crops. Winning this mission is a two-step process. First, you must completely enclose the settlement. This involves a long expanse of stone wall, so you must get the Quarry production up to speed immediately. If the compound is completely enclosed with stone, you will be able to survive the first few attacks by the Wolf's Swordsmen, even if you do not have sufficient Macemen or Crossbowmen to defeat the enemy in the field.

However, don't delay in setting up the weapons production line, because the final attack includes a large cadre of Swordsmen who make short work of the stone wall and Gatehouse. Until you receive the ability to produce crossbows, Macemen are the only hope against the Wolf's Swordsmen. You need a Tanner's Hut and of course, the tanners need cowhide, so you should build at least two Dairy Farms (one for cowhide and the other for food). Crossbowmen are the key to eliminating the Swordsmen, so we recommend three or more Fletcher's Workshops. Go ahead and build them early, so you'll be ready when the crossbow option appears.

Warning

Don't forget to go to each Fletcher's Workshop and "select" Crossbow for production. If you don't, the Fletcher will continue making regular bows.

Although you cannot win this mission without Crossbowmen, Macemen can hold their own if they have a large enough force. The ideal attack includes Crossbowmen firing from one direction while Macemen engage the Swordsmen in hand-to-hand combat. This is especially important during the final attack when Swordsmen hack away at the walls and gain entry to the castle. As their force dwindles, the Wolf's Swordsmen will take off and run through the settlement in every direction, so don't lose track of them toward the end of the battle. You cannot claim victory until you track down and kill each one.

12 THE RANSOM

Objectives

Acquire Gold: 6000

The spies report that the Snake has been ferrying gold into one of his counties where he is hastily erecting a castle. Launch a surprise attack to take his gold for yourself. We have sent along some Tunnelers to help you take the castle.

This mission includes the first full-scale siege. Although you can use the new Tunnelers to dig under the castle walls, you can pound the way inside just as quickly with a row of burly Macemen chipping away at the walls. You begin with a large invasion force of 42 Macemen, 10 Crossbowmen, 7 Archers, and 8 Tunnelers. The Macemen and Tunnelers provide the muscle for getting inside the castle, but while they work their magic, you must protect them, or the enemy Archers will turn them into mutton. The castle is southeast of the opening position. We recommend attacking the southwest corner of the castle, where the men will be hidden from the Gatehouse, and a safe distance from the closest Perimeter Turret. A rocky cliff lies west of the castle, and it provides an excellent vantage point for the Archers and Crossbowmen.

After they take out the enemy soldiers on the wall, turret, and Gatehouse, move the Archers and Crossbowmen up behind the Macemen as they break down the wall. Stay alert, because you will encounter more Crossbowmen and Macemen inside the castle.

After breaking into the castle, you discover 1000 pieces of gold in the treasury, but it is not nearly enough for you to meet the ransom. After repairing the damaged walls, examine the castle's economy, and make sure you have a robust food industry. Make sure you have at least two Fletcher's Workshops and two Tanner's Huts, so you can quickly field a sizable army of Crossbowmen and Macemen. The Snake is not happy about losing his castle, and with the Wolf's help, he will return with a powerful army. Deploy the Macemen to the southwest wall where they will knock down the enemy ladders before the enemy troops can reach the wall.

In between attacks, massage the tax rate to increase the flow of gold into the treasury. Balance the negative effects of increased taxes by doubling up on food rations. Of course, this will empty the Granary at a brisk rate; so don't forget to beef up the food production with additional farms, Bakeries, and Hunter's Posts. You need to place the farms outside the safety of the castle walls, so we recommend building protective walls to divert the enemy Macemen.

When each attack is over, focus on maximizing the food production to continually reward the population with extra rations. The best way to do this is to add additional processing outlets. For example, a single Wind Mill can support several Bakeries. Also, make sure you have multiple Dairy Farms, especially when the Tanner's Hut is using cowhides to make leather armor for the Macemen. Keep ratcheting up the tax rate to increase the flow of gold into the treasury. As long as you keep the popularity rating above 50, the workers will keep producing, and the money will flow. When you reach 6000 gold, celebrate another victory.

15 SNAKE EYES

Objectives

Kill the Snake

The Snake's new castle lies in a valley across from his old one! We have already occupied his old fort, build it up until you are strong enough to lay siege to the Snake's last castle to finish him for good. Should you succeed, pull out immediately as we don't have nearly enough men to take on the Wolf's main army. Raise some engineers to create the siege weapons you will need.

This mission presents an immediate challenge to finish, and reinforce a rambling, partially built castle in the southwest corner of the map. It is a logistical nightmare because of the large, irregular, area and the positioning of critical farming and quarry sites. Nevertheless, you must secure the perimeter before setting out to attack the Snake's new castle in the northeast corner of the map. And, you must immediately build an Iron Mine and Engineer's Guild to enable the construction of siege equipment.

The Pig provides the muscle while the Snake hides in his castle. His first attack is pitifully weak, but don't get overconfident. Subsequent attacks include increasing numbers of Macemen, and they are very destructive. If you cannot field a substantial number of Crossbowmen on the walls, be prepared for the enemy Macemen to come crashing through the gates. Once they make it inside the castle, you must respond quickly, or they will destroy everything in their path.

In between staving off the Pig's attacks, you need to build a strong squad of Engineers. When you have at least 7-8 Catapults, and a large force of Archers/Crossbowmen and Macemen, move out toward the Snake's castle. The Pig will keep attacking, even during the siege, so be sure to leave a strong garrison protecting the castle. When you reach the Snake's domain, focus the Catapults on the large Gatehouse and the wall to the left. Don't waste the time pounding the wall to the right of the Gatehouse, because even if you knock it down, a jagged section of cliff prevents the army from advancing.

Tip

Don't forget to "man" the Catapult after it is constructed. Each Catapult requires two Engineers before it is operational.

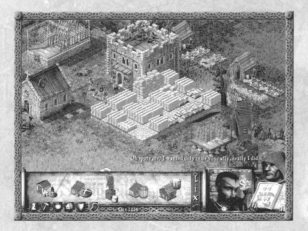

After destroying the first wall, you must still penetrate one more wall before gaining entry to the castle. Watch out for the Ballista in the left-hand turret. By the time you reach the inner compound, the Snake's forces should be severely depleted. Send several soldiers up to the keep to dispatch the Snake and win the mission.

14 THE MOUNTAIN PASS

Objectives

Eliminate All Enemy Units

The scouts report that there is a fort built into the mountain pass up ahead. If you fortify the garrison here, hopefully the Pig's horde will come to you. Our mysterious friends have sent more plans, this time for a large tower mounted Ballista. This should prove invaluable against the Pig's war machines.

After completing a successful siege in Snake Eyes, this mission focuses on defense. However, winning this mission requires more than a strong force of foot soldiers. You must use the Ballista to target enemy Battering Rams before they reduce the walls to rubble. Unlike some missions where the goal is to keep the enemy from breaching the walls, you can still win the mission by employing a strategy of retreat and fortify. Remember, the goal is to Eliminate All Enemy Units, so don't worry about the destruction around you; just concentrate on killing enemy soldiers.

This battle is fought on a rocky wasteland dotted with tall trees. The keep is located in the northwest quarter of the map. However, the enemy must first, fight its way through three fortifications, beginning with a Gatehouse, Square Tower, and Perimeter Turret located in the southeast quarter of the map. The rocks and cliffs limit the enemy's options, so you can focus all of the preparation on the first fortification. We recommend adding two or three layers of stone to the Gatehouse and surrounding walls. This will delay the enemy Battering Rams and give the Ballista operators more time to target them. When the rams are out of the way, the Archers can zero in on the remaining attack force and kill them before they can knock down the walls.

The next attack will likely overrun the first fortification. Drop back and fortify the second position. Expect larger waves of Crossbowmen and Macemen, and of course, more Battering Rams. It is critical to keep the Ballista operational, because they are effective at targeting Battering Rams.

> ### Tip
>
> It takes a long time to fashion leather armor, which is needed by Macemen and Crossbowmen. In this mission, it is critical to manufacture leather armor at breakneck speed. The only way to do this is to fill the available fertile land with Dairy Farms (it takes one cow to make three suits). When the Pig's forces break through the fortifications, the only hope is to counterattack with a strong army of Macemen and Crossbowmen.

It's more of the same at the next fortification. Do the best to strengthen the walls between battles and use the Ballista to take out the Battering Rams as quickly as possible. If the enemy Macemen break through, pull back and regroup at the next fortification.

Unless you defeat the Pig sooner, you'll make a final stand at the last fortification that guards the keep. Gather all of the Crossbowmen and position them atop the walls and turrets. They are the best long-range defense against enemy Crossbowmen and Macemen. Hold the Macemen in reserve, and if the Pig breaks through the walls, bring them into the fight. Always remember to surround the Lord with six Macemen at the top of the keep. It can be the difference between victory and defeat, if a few Macemen slip through at the end of the mission.

15 CARVING A PATH

Objectives

Eliminate All Enemy Units

Fight the way through the Pig's home county and escape into the fenlands on the other side. You will need to strike hard and fast before the Pig returns with his main force. Storm the gatehouse of the Pig's castle with a ram, dispatch the garrison and hide in the fenlands beyond.

The Pig's castle is very well defended, even without his main army. You must take out the turret defenders on the right-hand side of the castle first, before moving in with the Tunnelers and Spearmen. Pay special attention to the Crossbowmen and Archers in the two turrets surrounding the Gatehouse; their flaming arrow attacks are deadly. The Tunnelers can only dig on the darkened patches of rocky dirt in front of the castle. After they disappear into the ground, they tunnel under the closest tower, causing it to collapse. The Spearmen can fill in the Moat for the Battering Ram, or to provide a long stretch of wall for the Macemen to pummel.

Warning

Time is of the essence because of the Pig's impending attack. However, you must be careful not to move the Archers and Crossbowmen in too close, or they will be eliminated before they can complete their task of clearing the turrets. If you send in the Tunnelers and Spearmen before clearing the turrets, they will be quickly slaughtered.

It is important to protect the Crossbowmen, because you need them to clear the interior turrets. You must methodically attack one turret at a time, and while doing so, do not allow the Spearmen and Macemen to stand around inside the compound (or they will be easily killed). Instead, send several Macemen up into a turret while it is under attack from the Archers and Bowmen. When a turret is cleared, move the force up and repeat the procedure until all elevated positions are clear. Finally, take out the enemy Pikemen guarding the Barracks. When the last of the Pig's men is dead, victory is yours.

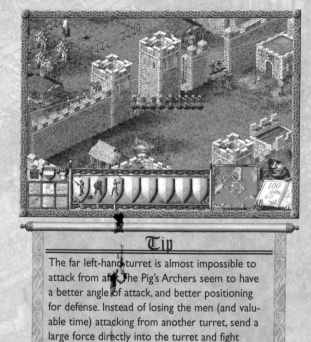

Tip

The far left-hand turret is almost impossible to attack from afar. The Pig's Archers seem to have a better angle of attack, and better positioning for defense. Instead of losing the men (and valuable time) attacking from another turret, send a large force directly into the turret and fight hand-to-hand.

16 FIGHTING RETREAT

Objectives

Acquire Goods: 200 Stone

Hold off against the Pig's attacks long enough to help the monks collect the stone they need, then make the retreat. The swamp is the biggest advantage here as a natural defense and as a source of pitch. The monks have told you about their "River of Fire" so use pitch ditches to good effect. This land is also favorable to the production of apples.

The swamp is the friend in this defensive-minded mission. The challenge is to hold off the Pig's soldiers long enough to gather 200 Stone for the Black Monks. The first order of the day is to place several Pitch Rigs over oil deposits in the swamp (look for wispy curls of white smoke). You'll need bushels and bushels of pitch, so be sure to place several rigs. Next, build two Quarries on the small rock deposit located along the western edge of the map. This is the only source for stone on the map, so you must protect it (a wooden palisade will do the trick). If the Pig's men slip through the defenses and destroy the Quarries, rebuild them immediately to keep the flow of stone to the Stockpile.

As we mentioned earlier, the best chance for victory is to utilize the natural defensive qualities of the swamp. At the beginning of the mission, you'll notice several dark, black areas in the swamp. These Pitch Ditches are highly flammable, and if you ignite them when the Pig's soldiers are in the vicinity, you'll be cookin' bacon for breakfast. At the beginning of the mission, there is an Archer in the tower just north of the swamp. If you target a Pitch Ditch, he will light his arrow using the brazier, and launch it to the target. The pitch ignites, and quickly spreads to adjacent areas. After you exhaust the initial supply of pitch, build new ones by clicking on the Pitch Ditch icon in the Castle Buildings menu. Hold down the mouse button and "paint" the swamp with pitch, by moving the cursor back and forth. As the Pig's attacks grow more intense, the Pitch Ditches become very important. Wait until several enemy soldiers are in the swamp, and then launch the flaming arrows. If you time the attack just right, you can wipe out a good portion of the Pig's army.

CHARACT

STRUCTURES

GENERAL STRATEGIES

COMBAT MISSIONS

ECONOMIC MISSIONS

MULTIPLAYER

MAPS

The most valuable military unit in this mission (other than the Pitch Ditch) is the Crossbowman. Build several Dairy Farms (for cowhide), and keep adding Crossbowmen as the weapons become available. Line the walls with Crossbowmen, and send 5 or 6 to the top of the Keep, where they can defend the Lord from long range. For added muscle, send several Black Monks to the Keep. These pious men of the cloth pack a mean wallop, and they hold their own against Macemen or Pikemen.

When the Pitch Ditches are set, and the walls are lined with Crossbowmen, you have all the necessary ingredients in place for victory. Stay alert, light up the swamp when the Pig attacks, and keep a close watch on the Quarries. When the Stockpile shows 200 Stone on hand, you will send the Pig home with his curly tail between his legs.

17 SMOKEY BACON

Objectives

Eliminate All Enemy Units

Use the resources you have gathered to rebuild and defend the ancient monastery. The army has left a clear path through the boggy grassland so it will not be long before the Pig finds you. Use Pikemen to block the Pig's troops and have engineers boil pitch. To maximize the effect, pour the boiling pitch on his troops from height.

This mission challenges the ability to multitask. You must rebuild the castle, and it will take some time, because it is a real mess. Add towers and turrets so the Engineers will have broad coverage with their boiling oil. All of this stone work requires a Quarry and several Ox Tethers. Place these structures early in the mission so you don't run out of stone. As for oil, you need several Pitch Rigs for raw materials. Just like in the last mission, the Pitch Rigs must be placed over oil deposits in the swamp. Finally, you need Oil Smelters to boil the oil for the Engineers. These pots must be strategically placed because the Engineers must run (or crawl) back to the Oil Smelter for a fresh supply of hot oil after each attack. If they have to travel too great a distance, the tower or wall will be unprotected while they collect their sizzling brew.

The Pig's army is well stocked with Pikemen. These heavily armored warriors go through most ground troops with ease, except for other Pikemen. Eventually, the Pikemen make their way to the Gatehouse, so you should have at least two Engineers (armed with oil pots) overhead. If you wait until several Pikemen are hacking away at the walls, you can fry them all with one drop.

Warning

Be careful where you drop hot oil. It is possible to start a fire that will spread and destroy friendly structures, like Farms or Hovels. For this reason, you should keep the area clear beneath towers and turrets.

The Pig keeps attacking with large armies of Macemen, Pikemen, and Archers. The existing Crossbowmen can take care of the Archers, but the Macemen and Pikemen are not so easy. Produce a large force of Pikemen, but keep them in the castle until the Engineers thin out the enemy force with hot oil. When you have the advantage, isolate and attack small groups of Pikemen, and then retreat back into the castle until the next opportunity arises. After a few attacks, the Pig snorts his disgust and concedes victory.

18 END OF THE PIG

Objectives

Kill the Pig

You have been charged to overthrow the Pig's final county by laying siege to his stronghold. You have besieged this castle before but it has since been rebuilt and now has a full garrison, so it will prove to be a far greater challenge. Our simple but direct approach last time with the battering ram may not now be enough. Build some siege towers to scale his tall walls.

As the briefing reminds you, this siege is going to be quite different from the last one. Instead of trying to beat the clock, this attack takes careful planning and perfect execution, because the Pig's entire army is waiting for you. There are several pieces of siege equipment at the disposal, including Siege Towers, for getting large groups of soldiers to the top of the walls, Battering Rams, for going through stone, and Tunnelers, for undermining castle towers. There are similarities to the last siege, in that you must fill in a portion of the Moat to provide access for the siege equipment. We still prefer the right-hand corner of the castle, because it is the area with the least amount of tower coverage. However, thanks to the flaming arrows, it is anything but easy.

First, move up a large squad of Macemen to guard the siege equipment. The Pig sends a steady stream of Macemen out to destroy them, and if you aren't prepared, you will lose the advantage. At the same time, move the Archers to an area just to the left of a rock outcropping, directly southeast of the castle's east-facing turret. From this point, the Archers can rain arrows on the turret, without taking return fire. Keep firing until all of the enemy Crossbowmen are eliminated. Then, move up slightly and take aim at the next turret to the left (don't forget the Archer with the brazier between the two turrets).

Now, it's time to use the Crossbowmen. Inch them over until they reach an area just to the left of the rock outcropping. Here, they can target the enemy Crossbowmen in the turret to the left of the Gatehouse, without suffering casualties from return fire. That's it for now; move the Crossbowmen back to a safe location. Next, bring the Archers back into the battle, moving them in a wide, safe, path to an area between two low hills, directly southwest of the left-hand turret. From here, they can nail the Crossbowmen in the turret.

When all of the turrets and flaming arrow Archers are gone, it's time to tackle the Gatehouse. Using the Siege Tower, deposit a squad of Macemen, Archers, and Crossbowmen on the wall next to the Gatehouse. After the Macemen take out the enemy Crossbowmen, get them Macemen out of the Gatehouse immediately, or the Pig's Crossbowmen on the interior wall will cut them to pieces.

Use the Battering Ram to pound through the interior wall, and send the Macemen to attack the first turret on the right. You should still have a substantial army of Macemen (at least 40 men), even after taking casualties during the storming of the Gatehouse. Continue moving back through the castle from turret to turret, clearing out the Pig's forces. When the Macemen secure a turret, occupy it with Archers and Crossbowmen, who will then fire on the next turret as the Macemen charge in from below. Eventually, the Pig will be all alone, and ripe for the taking.

19 PENNING IN THE WOLF

Objectives

Eliminate All Enemy Units

Pen the Wolf in by reinforcing the defensive fort we have started on the edge of his territory, then let his men come to you. They are likely to try to infect the people with disease so ensure you have contingencies in place for their arrival. Use Swordsmen and Mangonels to the best advantage.

You have many devices at the disposal in this defensive standoff against the Wolf. Place additional Pitch Rigs immediately, because you'll need a large supply to fill Pitch Ditches and supply Boiling Oil to the Engineers. Deploy Archers in the towers, and arm them with braziers. Spread Pitch Ditches throughout the area beneath the towers, and wait until the Swordsmen approach before engulfing them in flames. Try not to connect the outer Pitch Ditches or you will burn up everything too soon. A good technique is to create many u-shaped ditches with the points of the "U" facing the enemy. As a last line of defense, the area beneath the towers can be solid pitch, but don't set it off until you can take out a large army (wait until the Wolf's final all-out attack).

If you notice a green cloud hanging over the campfire, it is a poison spread by the Wolf. In fact, if you were paying attention, you would have seen a diseased cow flying over the ramparts. If you don't already have an Apothecary, now is the time, before the population succumbs to the Wolf's latest plague.

After three or four moderately challenging attacks, the Wolf gets bored and sends his whole army crashing down upon the castle. In preparation, train as many Engineers as you can, and line them along the walls and towers. By now, the Blacksmith's Workshops and Armorer's Workshops should be churning out heavy metal, giving you a substantial army of Swordsmen. As for the outer defenses, the Pitch Ditches won't stop the enemy in the last battle, so you'll need the Engineers to step up to the plate with their boiling oil. The goal is to keep the Swordsmen contained in the area beneath the towers for as long as possible. When the enemy bunches up next to the Gatehouse, light up the pitch for a major barbecue.

Also, you might want to add another Apothecary, because the diseased cows come raining down in bunches. The ending isn't pretty because the Wolf's army pretty much trashes everything in the castle. However, if you can keep the Crossbowmen and Engineers elevated long enough to inflict serious damage on the Swordsmen before they enter the castle, the garrison of Swordsmen should be able to mop up the remaining enemy soldiers and seal the victory.

Objectives

Eliminate All Enemy Units

Build up the forces and the castle itself and defend the current position until Sir Longarm arrives with reinforcements. You will be defending yourself against the Wolf's entire army in the biggest siege you have ever faced. Use knights to conduct sorties out of the castle.

Everything you've learned about defending a castle comes into play in this mission, except the scale is much larger. Fortunately, you have a good start on producing heavy soldiers, like Knights and Swordsmen. You'll need a massive army to hold off the Wolf long enough to receive reinforcements from Sir Longarm, but equally as important, you need to install a tight network of wall and tower defenses to support the troops. We're not talking about an occasional Engineer with a pot of boiling oil, either. If you want to survive this mission, you'll need an army of Engineers, Crossbowmen, and Archers, along with a closely knit patchwork of Pitch Ditches. You must pull out all the stops to keep the Wolf's army out of the castle for as long as possible.

While manning the defenses, you must churn out soldiers at a record pace, because the Wolf's final attack is overwhelming. Pick the spots and send squads of Knights out of the castle to disrupt the Wolf's advances. However, you should hold back a large army of Swordsmen and Macemen, but inevitably, the Wolf will end up in the backyard. Collapse the forces backwards, and make sure you have a strong protective army surrounding the Lord. The battle may get down to one final stand atop the keep, so don't want to be caught shorthanded.

21 FINAL VENGEANCE

Objectives

Kill the Wolf

Put an end to the Wolf using the combined forces of Sir Longarm and the king. You have vanquished the majority of his main army but the Wolf still has many men left and his stronghold is rumored to be impenetrable. He has discovered the secret of boiling oil so do not approach too quickly. Instead, make use of the new trebuchet to weaken him from afar.

If you haven't had a cow yet, now is the time, in the last mission of the Stronghold combat campaign. This mission introduces the Trebuchet, and yes, you can launch diseased cows at the Wolf's castle. But, first things first. The Wolf sends a welcoming party, so you must quickly move the Swordsmen and Crossbowmen to the head of the line, in front of the precious Siege Equipment. Assign them to defensive duty, and they will easily kill the attackers before they do any damage.

Now it is time to soften up the Wolf's exterior defenses. Using the Trebuchet, Catapults, Archers, and Crossbowmen, work the way back and forth around the castle, taking out the Archers and Crossbowmen in the turrets and towers. Along the way, the Catapult and Trebuchet should also cause a little damage to the walls. When you can safely approach the front of the castle, send in the Spearmen to fill in the Moat, and follow them up with the Battering Rams. The Spearmen may suffer some casualties from long-range flaming arrow attacks, but they will finish their job, allowing the Battering Rams to gain entry to the castle.

Move the Archers and Crossbowmen into the first yard, and take over the right-hand tower that is adjacent to the second Gatehouse. From here, take the time and target every enemy Archer or Crossbowmen who is in range. When the air is clear of flaming arrows, move the Battering Ram into place and punch the way into the inner compound.

Now you must contend with the Wolf's ground troops, and a nasty squad of Crossbowmen perched atop the keep. Move into the turret directly across from the keep. It will probably take two squads of Crossbowmen to stop the enemy arrows from flying. When the Crossbowmen are gone, you can target the Swordsmen who are protecting the Wolf. At the same time, send in some Macemen and Swordsmen to clear the remaining ground troops hanging around the turret. However, do not advance the foot soldiers to the keep! Another turret behind the keep is still garrisoned by flaming arrow Archers, and when they ignite the pitch in front of the keep, the men will be toast.

If you want to enter the keep and kill the Wolf in hand-to-hand combat, you'll need to clear out the rear tower first. However, you can also win the mission from the safety of the front turret. Just continue lobbing arrows at the Wolf until he falls to his knees. But, what fun is that? Instead, clear the rear tower and send every soldier in the vicinity up to the keep. When the Wolf begs for mercy at the tip of the sword, the final victory is yours. You are the new ruler of Stronghold!

Kill me now. I will not kneel before you.

SIEGE MISSIONS

These missions allow you to try the hand at defending some of the most famous castles in Europe, at various stages in their storied histories. Each mission is exclusively focused on combat, and as such, you won't have to worry about building, food, or any other economic concerns. Without an economy, you are limited to the forces on hand, so you must avoid losses as best you can, as they are not replaceable during the battle. The objective is simple: defend the castle against all aggressors to claim victory in these missions.

CASTELL Y BERE

History

Llywelen ap Iorwerth built this castle in 1221, after stripping his son of the territory of Gwynedd. Originally, the south tower was completely isolated from the rest of the castle by a rock-cut ditch, but it was later incorporated into the rest of the castle with extensions of the outer walls. The castle was one of the last to be surrendered to the English, and it was later retaken by Welsh rebels in 1294 under the leadership of Madog ap Llywelyn. It did not survive the subsequent battles with King Edward's armies.

DEFENDING

The entire fortress is built atop a large plateau overlooking the surrounding landscape, providing defenders with excellent visibility and defensive advantages. The South tower is best abandoned, as the enemy will opt for a direct assault on the front wall. Place all of the available archers in the front towers, the Gatehouse, and atop the wall. Focus the fire on the enemy Catapults at first, in an attempt to foil the enemy's ability to take down the walls. Once the assault begins in earnest, shift the fire to the advancing troops.

ATTACKING

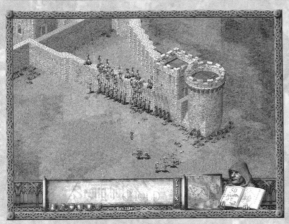

Battering Rams and advancing troops have trouble here, so attackers are well advised to bring ranged siege engines to support the attack. The eastern wall, just above the south tower, is an excellent point of attack for Laddermen. It is relatively isolated from the rest of the castle, and due to an improper angle, it fails to benefit from the full support of the other positions. This was often the case when modifications were made to the original design.

GLUECKSBURG

History

Located near the town of Flensburg, this castle is surrounded by a natural lake. It was built by master builder Nikel Karies between 1583 and 1587, and was home to several powerful dukes of Schleswig-Holstein. The Danes partially destroyed the castle in 1848 during the Schleswig-Holstein uprising. However, King Friedrich VII made it his summer home several years later, during which time it was refurbished.

DEFENDING

Gluecksburg is a defender's dream, because attacks can only come from one direction, and the line of attack is very narrow. Furthermore, the garrison can continually reinforce the main entrance wall of the castle because it is the only defense point. Unfortunately, the enemy catapults outrange the Archers, and you have no way of protecting the front wall. Rally all of the Archers atop the interior turrets, and decimate the enemy troops as they rush through the breach. With luck, you should be able to bring them down before they gain entry into the keep.

ATTACKING

No matter how you attack Gluecksburg, patience is a necessity, because a successful siege is likely to take some time. Since the castle sits in the middle of a lake, you can forget about tunneling, and filling in the lake would be a bit time consuming, to say the least. The lower walls between the center tower and corner towers are weak points if you can withstand the onslaught from above. Bring siege engines and try to knock a hole in the front wall. Continue to bring down the front wall, Gatehouse, and towers as long as the siege engines are operational. Once you've brought down the wall and towers, rush the keep with all of the troops for a victory.

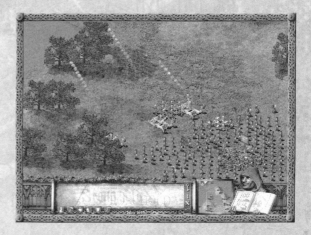

GUADAMUR

History

Guadamur is located about 8 miles west of Toledo, Spain. D. Pedro Lopez de Ayala built the castle in the late 15th Century. Toledo was capital for many invaders during the Dark Ages, before it came under Spanish control. The city was protected by a wall and castle during its time as Spain's leading commercial center of the 12th century. Guadamur was burned by French invaders in 1809, and restored in 1887 by the Count of El Asalto. The castle was again plundered in 1936 during the Spanish Civil War, and restored to its current condition some years later.

DEFENDING

The typical concentric castle of the 13th century was built with rings of stone walls. However, unlike Guadamur, the outer rings were so low to the ground and close to the inner castle, they did little more than keep siege machines a few feet away. Guadamur is a classic, square fortress with circular towers at each corner on the outer wall, and four taller square towers on the inner wall. The design is compact, so any attack will meet with heavy resistance from the towers. Rally all of the Archers in the front towers, and concentrate the fire on enemy siege engines to preserve the walls.

ATTACKING

Use siege engines to knock down the front wall, Even when a breach has been made, the job is just beginning, because the attack force then finds itself squeezed in between the walls. Do not send in the ground troops until you have created a breach in the inner wall. Once you have a direct line into the keep, storm the fortress with the melee troops. At the front of the castle, you'll find stairs that allow access to the upper towers and keep. Scale the stairs and clear the turrets if enemy Archers still give you trouble, and then take the keep for victory.

HEIDELBERG CASTLE

History

Heidelberg Castle overlooks the city of the same name from the eastern heights. It was constructed over the span of several centuries, beginning with a preexisting fortress of some kind being given to Conrad von Hohenstaufen by his half-brother, Frederich Barbarossa. In the following centuries the famed "red-walled castle" grew, although the end result is something of a hodgepodge of construction techniques and design elements that span a wide range of technical and stylistic influences.

DEFENDING

Heidelberg is better suited for hosting royalty in comfort than serving in its supposed primary capacity as a military fortress, a fact that is born out by the many defeats it suffered throughout history. On the defense, make every effort to repel an attack outside of the wall. You'll want more Archers than you have, so preserve them by monitoring the status of the towers they are stationed in, and evacuate them before they are destroyed when the tower is critically damaged. Station your melee troops in the courtyard unless the enemy brings Laddermen, in which case you'll need them on the walls to repel ladder attacks.

ATTACKING

The best attack is a massive assault on the front approaches, which are not steep. A minimal number of towers overlook the approach, allowing an invader to storm the walls with a high probability of success. Once across the wall, the lack of interior divisions ensures a quick end for the garrison, as any breach is very hard for the defenders to contain. Focus your energies on establishing that breach, and then pour through the walls with your entire force.

JAVIER

History

The rocky bluff that hosts Javier Castle was originally home to an Arab fortress in the 10th Century. Only the barest remnants of the original Arab structure remain, as it was later rebuilt and modified to reflect its Spanish masters, and stands today as one of the finest examples of Spanish architecture of the period. The castle is built on excellent high ground, and its fortifications are renowned throughout the region.

DEFENDING

Javier offers defenders a mighty position, and it can be held indefinitely with adequate troops and supply. The northern and eastern sides are protected by the rocky cliffs, and the walls of the fortress can stand up to incredible amounts of punishment on the bluff side. Concentrate the missile fire on the enemy Laddermen. If you start in on them early enough, you will destroy the entire ladder force, leaving the enemy to tediously pick through the walls with melee soldiers. Skewer them with arrows as they try.

ATTACKING

If you must attack this stronghold, gather the troops in the southwest corner of the map, and advance against the front side of the castle. Do not stray too far north, to avoid coming under fire from the towers that line the northwestern wall. Support the infantry with archers, and try a massed attack on the gatehouse.

LEEDS CASTLE

History

Leeds Castle was built as a Saxon manor in 857, and eventually became the stone castle of the Norman Crevecoeur family. Edward I built the fortified mill and barbican in 1278. The castle was used as a royal palace until falling to Edward II's troops in 1321, when he attacked the castle after the Queen was refused admission. This was the last siege in the castle's 1000-year history. Leeds Castle has been home to six medieval Queens of England. Lady Baillie, the castles last owner, purchased the property in 1926, and when she died, a perpetual foundation took over its care. Today the Leeds Castle gardens and museum attract thousands of visitors each year.

DEFENDING

You must get all of the troops to the front wall as soon as possible on the defense, as they begin the scenario spread all over the castle. If the enemy has brought a large number of siege engines, man only the towers, and abandon the outer wall once the towers are heavily damaged. Remember, you have multiple lines of defense at Leeds, and you should make the attacker pay in blood for every one. Hit him hard while he struggles to assemble an attack against each line of defense, and then abandon the positions just before he has enough combat power massed to take you. This delicate proposition takes a bit of balance, and if you are in doubt at Leeds, withdraw to the next line.

ATTACKING

Attacking Leeds is a very difficult proposition, and it is a classic candidate for siege. The moat does an excellent job of protecting the castle on all sides, and all attacks are limited to the impossibly narrow land bridge leading to the heavily fortified front gate. If you must engage in a direct assault, bring crushing amounts of missile troops to support a battering ram, or invest in several ranged siege engines. You'll need several rams, as the defenders can make pincushions out of them from the towers overlooking the entrance.

MONTERIGGIONI CITY

History

Monteriggioni is one of Italy's most famous walled cities, and stands today as a classic example of the Middle Ages in Italy. A total of fourteen towers ring the 570-meter long wall, which stands atop a natural hillside overlooking the Elsa and Staggia valleys. Two concentric sets of walls provide a garrison with a defense in depth, and the inner walls are even stronger than the outer walls.

DEFENDING

On the defense, focus the efforts on defending the inner wall. Harass attacking troops from the outer wall as they approach, and then withdraw to the inner towers, allowing the enemy into the outer ward. The outer wall should serve to separate the attackers somewhat as they filter over and through the wall, and you can pick them off with arrows as they make it across.

ATTACKING

On the attack, make every effort to conquer the outer wall en masse, spending as little time as possible in the no man's land between the walls. Be patient in the first phase of the attack, making a breach in the outer wall large enough to convey the bulk of the attack force in one large group. The steep hills prevent the siege engines from being effective against the inner wall, so don't overemphasize Catapults and Trebuchets. Once the outer wall is gained, move quickly against the inner wall with Laddermen and melee troops, while the own archers claim the outer towers to support the attack.

WARTBURG CASTLE

DEFENDING

A successful defense depends upon stopping the attackers from long range. There is no second line of defense, so all of the efforts must be made on the wall. Marshall the Archers into the northwest towers, avoiding the walls because of their vulnerability to siege engines. You must preserve the meager force of Archers, so abandon any towers that receive excessive damage before they fall. Concentrate the attacks on the greatest threats, which should be the enemy siege engines. If the enemy assaults with ladders, make every effort to destroy them before they are conveying troops up the walls.

ATTACKING

At first glance, attackers will have a difficult time figuring out how to plan a siege against Wartburg Castle. The long, narrow structure has 15 towers, but several of them are useless for defense, as they extend out from the main castle in a row. An attack is best staged against the long, straight wall. Although the towers provide excellent coverage for archers, the walls are not very high, and once into the inner courtyard, defenders have nowhere to hide.

WINDSOR 1070

DEFENDING

As noted above, Windsor is a traditional motte and bailey. Defend the outer ring as long as it is tenable, and then retreat to the motte above. The water features serve to channel the enemy attack into a few predictable avenues of advance, so focus the defense on those areas.

ATTACKING

On the attack, concentrate the forces and try to bring overwhelming force to bear on one side of the wall. You can use siege engines and archers to fire over the moat and water features, taking the defenders under flanking fire. Once the upper bailey is secured, mount a quick assault on the motte to avoid taking unnecessary losses in the killing grounds within the bailey.

INVASION MISSIONS

Invasion missions place you at the head of an army, either on the attack or defense of a stronghold. The missions vary widely in both scope and premise, offering you some of the most diverse challenges in the game. In some, you are faced with castle building and combat in the same mission, while others are purely combat missions with little or no economic concerns. These battles can be very challenging, but the following strategies will help you overcome the foes with skill and finesse.

DEFENDING THE HOMELAND

Objectives

Defend Stronghold Against Multiple Attacks

With the king gone but a few days, two of our adversaries have dispatched siege forces to probe the strength of our defenses. The king now has need of you earlier than planned. Make haste to the blasted heath to the south. There is a small castle there; bolster its defenses and hold off the enemy as best you can.

This mission is difficult, because you have limited economic options available to help bolster the defenses. Taxes are the only means of making money, as you cannot build a Marketplace. As soon as you take control, diversify the food supply with Dairy Farms. Place at least two inside the castle walls to maintain a food supply even in times of war. Additional Dairy Farms outside the walls help you build up a surplus, although they will likely be destroyed in a siege.

Tip

Gold is the limiting factor in this mission. Get a food surplus early, increase the rations, and then hike up the tax rate.

The Rat attacks from the south no less than four times, with each attack increasing in ferocity. He concentrates on the south and west walls, which host the gatehouses. Avoid constructing any new war engines, as you cannot produce the Engineers to man them. Instead, spend the gold on Fletchers and an Armory so you can produce additional Archers to aid in the defense.

To address the threat to the walls most often attacked by the enemy, fill in a portion of the moat on the southern corner of the castle by selecting the delete function ("X" on the toolbar) and clicking in the moat around the base of the corner. Fill in an area large enough to host a defense tower, and then knock down the corner of the wall to insert it. It should project outward from the corner on both sides, to give the archers an angle from which they can fire back along the outside face of the wall.

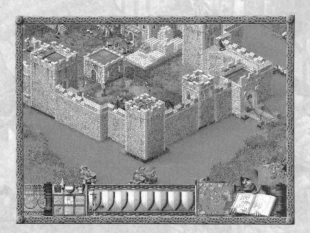

Replace the losses in between battles, and repair all damage to the walls. You should endeavor to avoid breaches at all costs. You begin the game with a stock of 15 pitch, which should allow you to create multiple pitch ditches along the outer edges of the moat. Rather than building them all at once or all together, spend a few points at a time digging small ditches. You won't need them at all for the first attack. Light them with flaming arrows from the braziers along the walls in the later attacks, but only when you are guaranteed a few kills by the enemy positions. Once consumed, replace the pitch ditches before the next battle, which will of course be larger still.

If you can hold on through the fourth battle, you'll win this mission. You need to have the Fletcher's Workshop up and running by the second invasion. Don't forget to recruit the Archers after their weapons are complete. You should have several Peasants available for drafting, but don't forget the importance of producing multiple food types to support the taxes.

THE FAT PIG (OINK, OINK)

Objectives

Acquire Goods: 3002 Bread

Defend Stronghold Against Multiple Attacks

The pig is back, bigger than ever, larger than life, and he wants the food!

You start this mission with very few assets, and only a short time to overcome a critical shortage of food and soldiers. To begin, place you Granary on the inside of the back wall, right next to the Gatehouse leading to the rear of the island. Bread is the only potential food source in this scenario, so you'll use the protected ground in back of the castle to host a slew of Wheat Farms. Start with four farms, which produce a healthy stock of Wheat by the time you get the Mill and Bakeries built. The Granary starts nearly empty, so immediately order half rations to stretch the supply as long as possible. Use a small bribe on the tax rate to offset the resulting resentment from the population.

Tip

While you wait for the next shipment of wood, use all of the pitch to dig fire pits along the front shoreline of the castle. Build three separate trenches, so that you can target specific troop concentrations without wasting all of the pitch.

Get four Woodcutters working as soon as possible. When they bring in their first boards, build a Mill and four Bakeries to staunch the flow of food from the Granary. Remain at half rations for now, to ensure an adequate food supply while you remain in crisis.

As soon as you can, construct an Engineer's Guild. You have ample starting funds to construct a Ballista, which will greatly aid in the defense of the castle. You begin the game with a measly two Archers in the employ, which is not nearly enough to repel even the first Pig attack. You'll eventually want a Fletcher's Workshop and Armory to add to the ranks of Archers, but they cannot be brought into play in time to help you repel the looming first attack. Place the Engineer's Guild inside the castle, and recruit two Engineers to man a Ballista in the south corner tower of the castle. Soon after, you'll be facing the first wave of Pig troops. Use the Ballista and Archers to smash the enemy Archers first, and their Spearmen will probably retreat.

After you recruit two Engineers, you'll find thyself out of available Peasants. Avoid the temptation to add another Hovel immediately, as a rabbit infestation will reduce the crop output in May, 1361. Continue at half rations until the food stocks have increased above 50 units. When you have adequate food stocks, add another Hovel, and then immediately add an Armory, Fletcher's Workshop, and Barracks to recruit new Archers.

At this point, you should be on the way to victory. Round out the bread industry with more Bakeries, and set extra rations. This will allow you to increase the tax rate, which in turn allows you to fund the military. Build another pair of Engineers and have them man a Ballista in the south tower outside of the castle. If you can afford it, a Mangonel in the second tower of the front wall helps you defend against subsequent attacks. Once you have adequate defenses, produce bread as fast as you can to win the game!

THE RAT'S REVENGE

Objectives

Acquire Goods: 50 Ale

Eliminate All Enemy Units

The nemesis, the Rat, wants another crack at you! Are you scared?

You start with a very mature castle, with its back set against the corner of the map. This is advantageous, because it gives you two borders that are absolutely secure against attack. Unfortunately, you start with little else: no infrastructure to speak of, and no soldiers. Set to work gathering food immediately, building a pair of Hunter's Posts and a few Dairy Farms. You can also build Apple Orchards down in the valley south of the castle.

Tip

Hit the spacebar to flatten the terrain when building inside the castle. This drops all buildings and terrain to the base level, allowing you to build right up to the edge of the map. You have plenty of room for farms inside the castle walls, keeping them safe from attack.

The Rat begins his attacks in December of the first year, so you must have an army prepared by then. You'll also need some troops early on to deal with a rampaging black bear that slaughters the Peasants if left alone. The Lord can be directed to attack the bear, and you should do so as soon as you see it near the castle.

Build a Barracks, Armory, and two Fletchers immediately. Supplement the Archers with a Mangonel and Ballista on the front towers, and build an Engineer's Guild to support them. By April, the Rat's troops will be upon you. Shut down the industries outside of town, and button up the castle as soon as the peasants are safely inside. You should have a small band of Archers by this point, which is just enough to repel the Rat's attack. Focus on the enemy Spearmen first, which pose the most immediate threat to the castle with their accompanying Laddermen. Once the Spearmen are gone, turn the attention on the enemy Archers.

135

After you repel the first Rat attack, concentrate on replacing the losses, and building up the population to support a larger army. The Rat attacks again soon, and you'll need approximately twice as many troops to repel the attack. Build a Poleturner's Workshop so you can recruit Spearmen to man the walls. A healthy bread industry is vital to the support of a larger population, and the diversification of food types will allow you to increase the taxes. Although the military treat is quite daunting in this mission, by focusing on growing the economy quickly and steadily you can muster a large garrison to repel the Rat's attacks indefinitely, thus buying you the time you need to produce the required 40 barrels of Ale. Don't build Inns, or they will consume the Ale you produce and prolong the mission.

THE VIPER'S NEST

Objectives

Kill Enemy Lord

The Snake has slithered back to the ancient fortress of his ancestors. Do you have the skill to traverse the maze of tunnels carved out by his forebearers and finish the odious reptile?

This mission places you in command of an invasion force, tasked with penetrating the canyon maze leading to the Snake's stronghold. Patience is the key in this mission. Although you are outnumbered, you can emerge victorious if you simply take on the enemy in bite-sized pieces. The enemy garrison is spread out all over the map, and most of the Snake's troops are strongly discouraged from leaving their posts, no matter what. Knowing this, you can inch the way across the map, engaging distant enemies one at a time with the archers while staying out of sight of their supporting troops.

The northern approach is the easiest. Stand the ground at first, and wait for enemy pickets to challenge you. Answer their hails with a volley of arrows, and then, cautiously set out down the northern path. The first encounter is with a small group of Macemen, supported by two Archers. Lead the way with a few Spearmen to draw the enemy missile fire, and answer with the own legion of Archers. When the first enemy Archer falls, the Rat Macemen will probably rush forward. Stand the ground, and turn the Macemen into pincushions before they reach the Spearmen. Next, round the corner and use the Archers to kill the remaining enemy Archer on the bluff.

The next challenge is a wall across the valley, followed by a gauntlet of enemy Archers. You can kill most of the guards at the wall with the Archers, and you can keep the odds in the favor down the valley by advancing slowly and cautiously, exposing the troops to as few Archers as possible at any one time. Again, lead with a few Spearmen to draw enemy fire, preserving the offensive power of the Archers.

Tip

The Engineers are valuable, because they can construct siege engines to aid you in the attacks. Use one to construct a Portable Shield, which will help you weather the enemy Archer's arrows. The others should create Catapults to give you the offensive edge as you attack down the canyons.

Before exposing thyself to the Gatehouse further down the valley, muster the Macemen for attack. Lead with a Portable Shield, and then assault the Gatehouse. Use the Archers to support the attack, resighting the Portable Shield to the Archers once the Macemen have reached the enemy Gatehouse. Keep the Catapults in reserve, to avoid damaging the Gatehouse. You'll want to capture it intact, because you can use it to weather the counterattack by enemy forces that will soon be upon you.

By now, the main garrison from the Snake's castle will be nearly upon you. Have the Archers quickly scale the Gatehouse, and deploy the Macemen before it. Close the Gate behind them to protect the Archers, and prepare for an extended counterattack. You should endeavor to hit the enemy with the Archers before they close into melee range. Use the narrow passages of the canyon to the advantage, funneling the multitude of enemy troops into a choke point, where they must fight a handful at a time.

Once you overcome the enemy counterattack, continue on the way to the enemy stronghold. The northern path is largely clear for the rest of the approach. Avoid the second Gatehouse and enemy tower on the extreme right of the map by diverting south at the last fork in the canyon. You'll pass by a few unmanned wooden palisades, and a few random archers. Take them out in the usual fashion, with the Spearmen and Portable Shield drawing fire.

Once you are near the castle, rush the Melee troops forward. Station the Archers on the bluff just north of the swamp, to expose them to only one of the enemy Ballistas. By moving the melee troops quickly to the wall, you minimize their exposure to enemy missile fire. Use the Archers to defeat the enemy Archers, and attack one face of the wall with all of the other troops. Once you gain entry into the courtyard, rush forward with the Archers while the melee troops head directly for the Snake Lord. The Archers will either draw fire away from the penetrating troops, or they will be able to enter the castle with no opposition. Once there, fire on the enemy Archers from the inside of the walls, where you have a much better chance to connect. Use the melee troops to slay the Lord and claim a victory for the side of good!

THE WEAK, THE BAD, THE FAT AND THE SLIPPERY

Objectives

Defend Stronghold Against Multiple Attacks

Four villains, four attacks, four times the trouble.

This mission puts you straight into action, and you have little time to gather the thoughts. Try pausing the game when you start the mission to get the bearings. You need a Granary, Barracks, and Armory immediately, to accommodate the goods you have at the beginning of the game. With these, you can recruit new soldiers to aid in the defense of the stronghold. After they are constructed, you have just enough wood to build three Woodcutter's Huts. Since there are woods so close to the castle, build these *inside* the castle walls, near the rear Gatehouse, to protect them from enemy attack.

With the economy jump-started, turn all of the attention to military concerns. You have an enormous garrison, but they are spread all over the map. Double-click on every unit you come across, and direct them to move to the central courtyard. As they begin flooding into the stronghold, start directing them to the front walls and towers, where they can help repel the Rat attack, which begins immediately. The Mangonels should concentrate their fire on the enemy siege engines, aiming for the center of their formation so that even misses have a chance at hitting nearby enemy troops. Continue to move the Archers into position as you engage the enemy, and direct them to attack anything in range. Combined, these efforts should be enough to repel the first invasion.

BASICS

CHARACTERS

STRUCTURES

GENERAL STARTEGIES

COMBAT MISSIONS

ECONOMIC MISSIONS

MULTIPLAYER

MAPS

With the first assault contained, spend a few moments repairing the walls and towers. Once that's done, scan again for any stray troops, and continue to deploy them along the front wall. Keep all of the melee troops in reserve, ready to man the walls just in case enemy troops manage to scale them. Replace any pitch ditches you used in the first assault, focusing on those areas of the wall that may have been breached.

Bolster the economy, increasing food productivity, population, and resource exploitation as much as possible. You can build behind the castle freely, as all enemy attacks originate in the southwest. Make sure you have a Quarry and Ox Tether operating to gather stone, which will enable you to effect repairs on the castle between each battle. As the mission progresses, you should be progressively *more* prepared for each battle, not less. The position is strong and the enemies are channeled along one narrow attack corridor, so as long as you provide for the economic growth and stability, you should have no trouble defeating all of the invasions.

WHO'S AFRAID OF THE BIG BAD WOLF?

Objectives

Defend Stronghold Against Multiple Attacks

Who's afraid of the big bad Wolf? You should be! In this deadly mission, he's coming for you with everything he's got!

This is perhaps the ultimate invasion mission. You begin with a fertile, open map, with abundant resources of all kinds and access to every facility in the game. Place the stronghold somewhere along the northern edge of the map, to secure the back against attack. The enemy attacks repeatedly from the south, and if you are nestled up against the map edge and/or impassable terrain, you can funnel the enemy attacks down the killing fields of the choosing.

Plan the settlement as a military fortress from the ground up. Pause the game and look over the map, planning the ramparts and fields of fire before laying down the first building. The northwest corner of the map is an excellent candidate for the stronghold's site, as it butts up against impassable bluffs to the rear, while offering you close proximity to several resources. The northeast corner is similar in security, but it has the disadvantage of being far displaced from the most commonly used goods of wood and stone, essential for castle construction.

You may wish to take an alternate approach, and focus on containing enemy attacks before they have a chance to develop. In this case, build a small keep in the interior to protect against penetrations, and build massive defenses on the heights that belt the southern edge of the map. These badlands channel enemy attacks, allowing you to build multiple layers of defenses along narrow channels. This approach takes advantage of the natural terrain, but it can prove too weak to withstand the first attacks, and it is vulnerable to enemy penetration into the settlement before you have all the choke points covered with multiple layers of defenses. Still, if you are efficient in the first few minutes of the mission, you can establish a meaningful defense in the passes and weather the first attack successfully.

Pour everything you can into the economy for the first year of the game. Focus all of the efforts on building the largest, healthiest settlement you can, and completely ignore defensive considerations. Build multiple food production industries, and gather wood and stone in abundant quantities. As you expand further, start producing pitch and iron for the defense. Manage the coffers with a balance of food variety, extra rations, and taxes.

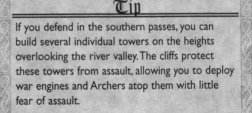

Tip

If you defend in the southern passes, you can build several individual towers on the heights overlooking the river valley. The cliffs protect these towers from assault, allowing you to deploy war engines and Archers atop them with little fear of assault.

When you reach 1067, switch over to military preparations: build a Barracks, Armory, Fletchers, and Poleturners. Construct the walls out of whatever materials you have available. At least a wooden palisade should surround the inner settlement no matter what; you can upgrade to stone later on. Begin to muster troops as soon as possible, with a target of a dozen Archers and a handful of Spearmen. You may also have time to create an Engineer's Guild to produce a few Ballistas or Mangonels, if you have towers to host them.

The Wolf's assaults grow stronger over the years, but so should the defenses. Line the southern passes with ever-deeper series of walls and Gatehouses, and dot the hilltops with towers to rain death upon the hapless enemy as he struggles to assemble his invasion forces. As the population grows, you may wish to introduce religion to the masses as a way of boosting Popularity, which will allow you to tax them more heavily. Continue the economic expansion as you expand the military, and the Wolf eventually exhausts himself on the impenetrable walls, handing you the ultimate victory.

BASICS

CHARACTERS

STRUCTURES

GENERAL STRATEGIES

COMBAT MISSIONS

ECONOMIC MISSIONS

MULTIPLAYER

MAPS

Chapter 7

ECONOMIC CAMPAIGN

Stronghold's Economic Campaign challenges you with five peaceful scenarios centered on one or more specific economic goals. Some missions task you with constructing a certain number of buildings, while others challenge you to amass a target amount of goods or resources. Whatever the mission goals, you conduct the operations in peace, without threat of military attack. You'll still have need for swordplay in some of the missions, however, as wild animals can sometimes be a nuisance—or even a deadly threat.

VICTORY FEAST

Objectives

Acquire: 100 Cheese

Acquire: 12 Ale

The royal court is soon to host a great banquet. We need you to found a small village for the production of ale and cheese. Find a clearing in the woods to the south of the King's castle and get to work immediately.

The first task is to place a Keep (a Saxon Hall in this mission), which is the center of the settlement. In the Economic Campaign, the most important feature of the Keep is the attached Stockpile. The Stockpile stores wood, crops, and all other inedible goods. All workers producing non-food items must deposit their goods in the stockpile, which means it should be in a central location to shorten their trips. By doing so, their walking time is minimized, which results in more time spent producing goods for the economy. There is a large clearing amongst the trees in the center of the map that makes a perfect site for the Keep.

Tip

This mission begins with a massive stockpile of wood. Don't worry about building Woodcutter's Huts in the early game, as the wood stocks will last through almost the entire mission.

The Granary is next, for food storage. The placement of the Granary has different criteria than the Keep. It should be placed close to the main food production areas of the settlement, to minimize travel times for the food industry workers. It should also be somewhat close to the Stockpile, as the bread industry requires Bakery workers to take flour from the Stockpile and deposit finished bread in the Granary. Dairy Farms are central to this mission, and they must be constructed in open fields. Build the Granary to the left of the Saxon Hall, just inside the tree line bordering the plains.

Now, make sure the peasants have enough to eat. Build Hunter's Posts to the north, south, and east of the Granary. The Hunter's Posts should be built facing opposite sides of the map to take maximum advantage of the migrating game herds. Place them no more than 20 squares away from the Keep (about five times the width of the Granary) so that the Hunters don't have to walk too far to deliver their prepared food. However, be sure to place them beyond the open plains, to leave room for the Dairy Farms.

Build five Dairy Farms immediately. Once they are operating, there should be ample food production, but there is a short lag time between construction and the start of production. As soon as the Farmers are delivering their first loads of cheese, build another Hovel to attract additional citizens. Put these immigrants to work in five more Dairy Farms, plus a Woodcutter's Hut to begin slowing the depletion of the wood stocks. With ten Dairy Farms in operation, there shouldn't be any problem producing 100 cheese.

You'll now be ready to build another Hovel for more population. Once established, build two Hops Farms and two Breweries. These two buildings are interdependent: the Hops crop is put in the Stockpile, where it is taken to the Brewery and turned into ale. All of these buildings should be placed near the Stockpile. At this point, victory is close at hand, with the ale flowing in and cheese aplenty in the Granary. If you wish to speed along victory, build another Hovel to support another pair of Hops Farms and Breweries, along with four more Dairy Farms.

THE LONG VALLEY

Objectives

Acquire Weapons: 12 Bows

Acquire Weapons: 8 Swords

The king's armory is depleted. Go to the valley to the east of the castle and begin weapons production. The fertile valley floor is ideal for apple growing which you can use to feed the people. A local trader here trades in iron, which you can buy to produce some of the weapons needed.

This mission teaches some of the basic concepts of the trade system in Stronghold, which is accessed via the Market building. Only limited types of goods are available on any given map, and demand is also unique to a given mission. In this case, it's possible to sell food, and buy iron.

Place the keep to provide reasonable access to the wood in the southwest corner of the map while still staying reasonably close to the Apple Orchards you'll plant in the river valley. Build the Granary on one of the hills next to the river valley to put it near the future orchards without sacrificing any of the fertile ground.

Place three Woodcutters adjacent to the trees, on the path the Woodcutters must take back to the keep. After they are constructed, turn the attention to the bears that roam the river valley. This is perfect ground for the Apple Orchards, but the farmers will be mauled by bears if they settle the valley. Dispatch the Lord to the area, and kill one of the bears. Soon after, you'll be joined by some of the bandits living out in the woods, and they will help clear the area of bears. Wolves will also threaten the settlement, but the newly allied archers can protect the people.

With the bears at bay, concentrate on Apple Orchards. Build as many as possible, as often as you can. Every time there's enough wood, build another orchard, until there are at least 10 Apple Orchards producing plump red fruit in the vast apple empire. You'll eventually need to build another Hovel to house more workers. At this point, there should be a great surplus of apples, enabling you to reward the populace with Extra, or even Double Rations. Choose a setting that keeps the food inventory breaking even from month to month.

Tip

To adjust the rations, click on the Granary. The interface bar on the bottom of the screen displays a pointer with various plates of food around it. Click on the plates to change the rations doled out to the subjects.

Charity is not the central motivation for doubling the subjects' rations. The extra food results in increased popularity, which soon peaks at a maximum score of 100. As soon as you approach this number, hike the taxes by clicking on the keep, and then adjusting the tax slider to the right. It's possible to balance the unhappiness penalty with that earned by the surplus rations and bring in extra gold without upsetting the population.

After fiddling with the rations and taxation, there should be some wood stored up. Build a Market, and begin selling the surplus apples for gold. Spend the money on iron, for use in the production of the bows and swords required for victory. A total of twenty units of iron are needed, which is four individual purchases. Build a few more Apple Orchards to increase the pace of the earnings, but be sure to leave three peasants available for employment, two in Fletcher's Workshops and the other in a Blacksmith's Workshop.

When there are enough materials saved up, construct the weaponsmith buildings, along with an Armory to store the completed weapons. They should all be near each other, and placed next to the Stockpile for access to the iron stored there. At that point, it's merely a matter of waiting for the weapons to build up to the required levels for victory.

GATHERING THE HARVEST

Objectives

Achieve Population: 100

Acquire Gold: 3200

We now need to establish a small town to provide grain for the castle. The plains to the west of the castle should provide an ideal location. Go there and get the town up and running.

The introduction of the bread industry is the most notable feature of this mission. Bread is, in fact, the most productive food industry in Stronghold once it's up and running, but it takes a long time to get from plowed wheat fields to baked goods. For this reason, the opening minutes of this mission are especially critical. Get the bread industry up and running before the initial food stocks run out.

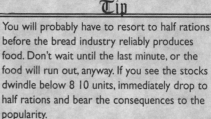

Tip

You will probably have to resort to half rations before the bread industry reliably produces food. Don't wait until the last minute, or the food will run out, anyway. If you see the stocks dwindle below 8 10 units, immediately drop to half rations and bear the consequences to the popularity.

First, build the keep in the very center of the open fields on the southern side of the map. This leaves ample room around the Stockpile for the placement of Wheat Farms. When the wheat is ready for harvest, it must be gathered and taken to the Stockpile as quickly as possible, or it will rot in the fields. This requires several trips back and forth, and if the distance is too great, much of the crop will be lost. Therefore, reserve the entire area immediately surrounding the keep for the placement of Wheat Farms. Also, add another square to the Stockpile immediately, to accommodate the high goods production. It's free, and it's harder to do later in the game, when dozens of workers are crisscrossing the area.

Place the Granary a moderate distance from the keep, so that a Wheat Farm and a few rows of Bakeries fit in between the Granary and Stockpile. If you care to count, roughly 20 map squares should be sufficient distance between the Stockpile and the Granary.

The next objective is to build three Woodcutter Huts, a Mill, and a Bakery and Wheat Farm. A Mill is the middle link in the bread industry chain, turning harvested wheat into flour for bread. Place it just outside the area reserved for Wheat Farms, in a direction other than the one leading to the Granary. Since the Mill workers never interact with the Granary, there's no reason to take up space along that precious corridor with the Mills.

Tip

Pestilence will occasionally devastate the standing wheat crop. Maintain a surplus of wheat in the stockpile by having one or two extra Wheat Farms in operation at all times, and you'll never notice the effects of these disasters.

The Bakery should go in between the Stockpile and Granary. Build nothing but Bakeries with available wood until there are five in operation, and then expand the food industry with additional Wheat Farms and Windmills. Unlike the ale industry, the bread industry does not work on a 1:1:1 ratio. Each Windmill serves approximately three Wheat Farms and five Bakeries, so build accordingly.

Soon, you'll need more population to support the expanding industry. Wait until you have at least a 6-month supply of food at the current population level, as well as about 40 units of wood to allow a rapid expansion of the bread industry to support the increased population. Each time you grow, invest most of the new population in more bread production, maintaining the 3:1:5 ratio as you expand. Build more Woodcutter's Huts as you expand as well, to support the increasing rate of construction.

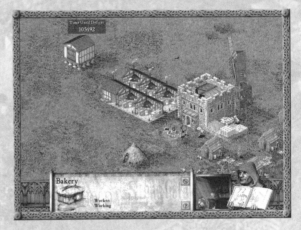

Manage the money by taxing the population, offsetting the popularity penalty with increased rations. You can also create an ale industry, selling the liquor instead of distributing it at Inns. As the population expands, you'll find it easier and easier to come by large sums of cash from taxes, and since there are no financial obligations other than 3200 gold for victory, simply stockpile the wealth. Grow steadily and quickly to meet the population goal before time runs out to claim a victory in this mission.

A DETERRENT

Objectives

Acquire Goods: 350 Bread

Acquire Goods: 180 Stone

Acquire Goods: 40 Leather Armor

Acquire Goods: 40 Maces

Complete Castle

Our scouts have spotted raiders to the north. We have started building a castle into the mountain pass north of here. Take charge of the construction and finish the castle to block their approach.

This is the first real castle building experience in the Economic Campaign. You begin the scenario with a partially completed fortress. Although the first temptation might be to get a Quarry started to continue construction, see to the needs of the population first. Build three Woodcutter's Huts, and follow up with two Hunter's Posts and two Apple Orchards, just outside the walls.

Immediately upon beginning the mission, begin iron production. This is essential to a victory on this mission. Without an early start on iron production, there will be no way to attain the required amount of maces in time.

Use the first influx of wood to build up food production. Design a bread industry around a single Windmill within the walls, with its corresponding Bakeries and Wheat Farms. A good castle always has some provision for producing food within its walls, to minimize the impact of a siege on the garrison's food supply. Continue expanding the food industries with Dairy Farms and additional Apple Orchards until ample stocks of food are coming in, and then turn the attention to completing the castle.

Tip
Leave room for one or two extensions to the Granary, as acquiring a stockpile of bread in this mission is necessary. Also, large quantities of goods are going to be dealt with, so immediately expand the Stockpile by one or two squares.

Add a Quarry in the granite field in the northeast corner of the map. Put it in the very corner, so that it's possible to build more Quarries later. An Ox Tether will also be required, to service the animals that bring the quarried stone back to the Stockpile. The placement of the Ox Tether doesn't matter very much, so long as it is on the way from the Quarry to the stockpile.

The towers and layout are already fairly established, and you have only to build walls between them to complete the castle. Gatehouses on the side walls are not entirely necessary, but they will lower the travel time for the peasants. As the workforce expands with the construction of new Hovels and Houses, remember to increase the food production with more and varied foods.

You'll eventually find the food supply well in hand, and at that point, be ready to expand the quarrying operations. Build additional Ox Tethers and Quarries to get the stone flowing to the Stockpile. Build the northwest corner of the castle last, so you can keep the stone coming into the Stockpile along the most direct path, for as long as possible. Once you connect all four sides, the castle is considered complete. Satisfy the other mission requirements, and you'll be victorious!

> ### Tip
> The Perimeter Turret is one third less expensive than the Defense Turret, but it is not as strong. The Defense Turret has better protection all around, and does not suffer from the same vulnerability to tunneling that haunts the smaller turrets.

A CASTLE IN THE MARSH

Objectives

Acquire Gold: 5000

Finally, we need to replenish the castle treasury. We have a contract to supply pitch to a foreign buyer. Go to the old castle in the marsh and expand pitch production. A cruel master has ruled the people there. It is up to you whether you continue his policies or adopt a kinder approach.

The full range of castle elements is available in this mission, and you are challenged to use each one to its best possible benefit. The scenario begins with a completed castle, but the popularity is an abysmal zero. The first thing to do is to make sure the people are eating. The second thing is to overcome that big red zero popularity, so that in the months to come you actually *have* people around to feed.

Begin the mission by establishing the basic industry. Build three Woodcutter's Huts in the corners of the map to start bringing in wood for all of the upcoming construction projects. Skip placing a hut in the corner opposite the Gatehouse, because that would require the Woodcutter to walk all the way around the castle wall to drop off his wood. Later, you'll probably want to install a second Gatehouse in the back wall to open worker access to the fertile ground behind the castle.

Next, build Hunter's Posts, Apple Orchards, and Dairy Farms to equalize the food production and consumption. Once you're feeding the population reliably, diversify food production into the bread industry, which is capable of feeding many more mouths. Be careful not to rely entirely on bread, however, because occasional blights can devastate the entire wheat crop. If you maintain Stockpiles of flour, you can absorb such calamities without adverse effects on the food output.

Addressing the popularity problem is a more complicated proposal. There are several options. Although choosing to continue to rule with an iron fist is an option, it's still a requisite to get the popularity above 50, or the subjects will gradually desert the castle in search of nicer communities. The former Lord of the castle ruled with a heavy *fear factor*, which increases worker efficiency through the threat of punishments such as stocks, gallows, racks, and dungeons. Naturally, a high fear factor means a low popularity, but worker output is increased by up to 50%.

The popularity penalty incurred by the presence of punishments can be offset through increased rations, working Inns, and religion. This is the first time that access to religious buildings is available in the Economic Campaign, and their availability is a great opportunity to gain popularity. Religious buildings come in three sizes, beginning with the small Chapel, and moving to the larger Church and finally the massive Cathedral. Each religious building can bless a limited number of peasants relative to its size, so as the population grows, more and larger religious buildings are needed to maintain the same level of religious coverage (and resulting popularity bonus).

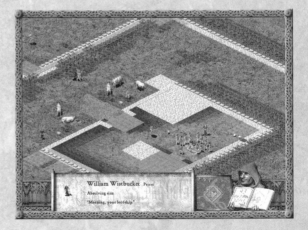

Another option is to overcome the negative popularity by reducing the castle's Fear Factor. There are over a dozen implements of terror throughout the map, from the Dungeon in the outer courtyard to the Chopping Block next to the Granary (how disgusting!) and a Burning Stake deep in the surrounding marsh. If you wish to loosen the chains around the ankles of the inhabitants, delete these punishments by clicking on the "X" in the interface bar, and then click on each item you wish to remove. Don't miss the Gallows, which are spread out all over the map, several of which are hidden behind walls. Rotate the map through a full circle to make sure you've eliminated everything. As soon as you've eliminated the punishments, you'll see the popularity start to rise immediately.

After eliminating all of the punishments in the lands, take the quest for popularity a step further by building beautification elements and recreational facilities. These items are available in the Town construction menu, under "Good Things". Clicking on the Good Things box brings up an assortment of structures that increase the popularity. However, be warned: each structure reduces the efficiency of the workforce, as they take more and more leisure time to enjoy these structures instead of working.

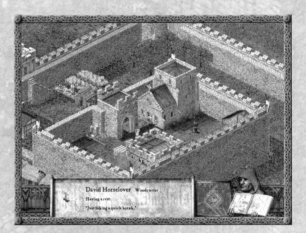

Unless you wish to levy extremely high taxes or seek a very large population, Good Things are not usually necessary to maintain a popularity rating of 100. However, since the objective in this scenario is to gather money, they represent viable options. If you choose to use them, hold off on their construction until you have surpluses in all the industries, because the loss of work efficiency translates to less output. Lowered output on a critical industry like food production could mean the difference between producing surpluses and starving!

Continue to build the community smoothly and steadily, selling surpluses at the market for

> ### Tip
> Use the scribe's Popularity Report to manage the rate of change in the popularity. The line at the bottom that reads "In the coming month" displays the sum of all factors affecting the popularity.

gold. Pitch is the best money-earner, at 30 gold per unit. Build up the popularity bonuses of the choosing to get to 100 popularity, and then raise taxes until the popularity is holding steady. At this point, it should only be a matter of time before the taxes and exports earn you the required 5000 gold, ending the Economic Campaign in a glorious and wealthy success!

ECONOMIC MISSIONS

The Economics Missions are an assortment of stand-alone challenges based around one or more economic goals. They tend to be more challenging than the campaign missions overall, so you should consider tackling the Economics Campaign before taking on these individual missions. As with the campaign, there won't be any enemies to encounter in these missions other than the clock, empty coffers, and the hungry mouths of the subjects.

A REQUEST FROM THE KING

Objectives

Acquire Weapons: 8 Swords

Acquire Weapons: 8 Bows

In readiness for his forthcoming crusade, the king has ordered that the royal armory be restocked. Forthwith, the fiefdom is to supply his majesty's steward with a quantity of weapons. You are to have the shipment of weapons ready for dispatch before the king and his army set forth. A local trader here sells iron, which you can buy to produce some of the weapons needed.

This mission is quite similar to the second mission in the Economic Campaign, except this time, you have a time limit! The allotted time is quite short, so concentrate on making the most efficient use of the available resources. Since there are very few trade or production options in this scenario, the only hope is to fill the coffers with taxes, and then use the funds to buy iron for weapon production.

Tip

Try slowing down the game speed during the building phases of time-sensitive missions. You'll find it's much easier to build efficiently when time isn't flying by. Conversely, feel free to speed up the game when you're waiting for new resources to come in.

Start by building the Keep on the extreme left side of the southern plateau. This will situate it near several stands of trees for wood gathering, while preserving the limited fertile ground on this map for Farms. The Granary should go directly in the valley on the extreme east side of the same southern bluff, which places it between the fields on the bluff and the farmland in the river valley.

Get three Woodcutters up and running in trees around the keep. With wood coming in, turn the attention to the food supply. Use the fertile ground on the center and eastern islands to host three Apple Farms, building outward from the Granary. Put three Dairy Farms on the southern plateau next, which will give the food stocks an early boost in anticipation of increasing the population. The Popularity will also benefit from the increased diversity in food types, which will allow you to tax the population more heavily without detriment.

When the Woodcutters start producing, construct a Market. This will allow you to trade for Iron, and sell Apples for profit. Buy 10 iron (click twice on "Buy"), and then leave the Market. There should be 300 gold left, which is enough to build a Fletcher and a Blacksmith. Construct an Armory between them, to host the weapons they produce. Situate this entire weapons industry near the Stockpile, so that the weaponsmiths have easy access to the iron stored there. Once you've completed these steps, the weaponsmiths will start work on the required implements of war immediately.

At this point, the dairy production should have kicked in, allowing you to increase to Extra Rations at the Granary. The additional food will keep the peasants happy, allowing you to instate Average taxes. As soon as you have enough wood, build additional Apple Farms, as well as one or two more Dairy Farms. You should have about 50% more Apple farms, so that you can sell the profits at the Market. Dairy goes straight towards feeding the population, so you don't need to produce excess.

Build the extra housing needed to support the expanding Farms. The primary goal is to use increased rations to offset the drop in popularity caused by increased taxes. The taxes are necessary to purchase the iron you need to buy for weapon manufacture, and also for the construction of additional weaponsmiths. Keep a safe amount of food stockpiled, as the cows and apples will both suffer from maladies in the mid-game. If the stores are sufficient, you will not be affected by the events.

It should be just about the beginning of the second year of the scenario at this point. Build a second Fletcher and Blacksmith near the Armory. You may have to increase taxes to High in order to get the money together, which will cause a gradual decline of the popularity. You will be fine as long as it stays above 50, so concentrate on pulling in gold as fast as you can. Remember to sell apples for profit, as well. With two of each kind of weaponsmith working by the beginning of the third year, you'll have no problem meeting the deadline. Remember to purchase 10 more iron to keep the smiths in supply. You'll need about 500 gold for this, so start saving early!

BLESSING THE PEASANTS

Objectives

Achieve Population: 100

Blessed Percentage: 90

Fear Factor: Pleasant (3)

To confirm the status as the most pious of the king's lords, you need to ensure that every single one of the serfs attends church.

This mission is much easier than the first one, thanks to the open-ended timeframe you have to achieve the goals. The ultimate aim is to have a large, church-going population. Since you will be building plenty of churches, site the Keep on the left side of the map, on the heights near the stone field in the upper left corner. This will minimize the round trip time for the Oxen as they haul the stone to the Stockpile. Put the Granary on a hilltop near large, flat fields, so that the farmers won't have far to go to drop off their crops.

You must first feed the peasants' stomachs before you can feed their souls. To this end, build a few food-producing buildings before carrying on with the work of the Almighty. Apple Orchards and Dairy Farms should go next to the Granary to get you started. Reserve the fertile valley floors for Apple Orchards, which cannot be placed on the hilltops. Use those higher areas for the less fickle cattle.

You need churches to bless the peasants, and you need stone to build churches. After you've placed the first Hovel due to population demand, start up the stone quarrying industry with a Stone Quarry in the rock field on the left side of the map. Build two Ox Ties right next to the Quarry, so the stonecutters don't have to carry the stone very far on their own. If you place the Quarry on the extreme corner of the rock field, you'll have room for two, in case you wish to increase the production later in the mission.

Tip

If you want to speed up the income, you can build a Pitch or Iron industry in the northeast corner of the map. Simply extract the resources and sell them at the Marketplace for a tidy profit that will help speed along victory.

A Market will allow you to manage the economy quite comfortably, so build one as soon as you can spare the wood. Sell the production surpluses, and buy meat to maintain a diverse diet for the subjects. The resulting popularity will allow you to charge higher taxes, which in turn will give you more buying power for new churches. As you increase the church coverage, you'll experience additional popularity bonuses, which will allow you to increase taxes even further.

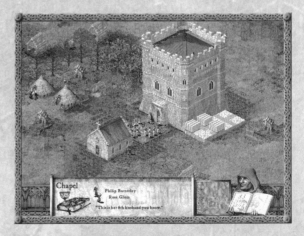

Invest heavily in the bread industry as the population grows. You'll find it increasingly difficult to maintain a diverse diet as the peasants are consuming more, but you can buy supplemental food at the Market. Expand the Granary to accommodate the larger volumes of production and consumption, and maintain a cushion in case a disaster should affect food production. Build the Good Things last, as these will lower the productivity of the subjects and slowing growth. When the population is nearing the target level of 100, focus on church building to get the blessed percentage up into the required range for a victory.

THE EMERGING CITY

Objectives

Achieve Population: 300

Acquire Gold: 10000

Blessed Percentage: 30

Drinking Percentage: 80+

Fear Factor: Pleasant (5)

You have a long time span to turn the village into the greatest economy in the land.

Although the mission briefing suggests a time limit, there is none, so the way to win is through steady, consistent building. You have access to a full Marketplace in this mission, so you should make the most of the abundant natural resources on this map by exporting manufactured goods for profit. Site the Keep in the center of the map, tucked into the nook between the central forest and the hill that contains the iron deposits.

Tip

Watch out for the bear that roams the map. As soon as you spot it, select the Lord and direct him to slay the beast. Left alone, the bear will slaughter the cattle and peasants.

This mission is almost like a free build map, and it requires a whopping 300 population to win. Use every method at the disposal to increase the popularity and tax the population. With ample resources and a large tax base, the money isn't the biggest challenge in this mission, it's supporting such a large population. Use diverse food industries and maintain ample stocks. You'll end up needing as many as 8 Granaries to hold all of the surplus food stocks, because you'll be producing (and consuming) such massive quantities. Plan for this by leaving room around the original Granary for later expansion.

Unless you are looking for an extended, leisurely mission, don't bother building defenses on this map, even though they are available. As with all of the Economic Missions, you face no threat of enemy attack, and the resources will be better spent by reinvesting in the infrastructure.

Religion and Good Things will help bolster the popularity, allowing you to increase the tax rate for even greater economic vitality. Use Good Things as a last resort, as they will lower the population's productivity and thus require a larger population to support the same amount of production. Make sure you maintain an adequate variety of food, especially in the later stages of the scenario. In particular, you will probably find that you'll have to import a great deal of meat in order to maintain the varied diet of the populace. With a happy, productive population, you should have no trouble winning this scenario.

THE FOREST

BASICS

CHARACTERS

STRUCTURES

GENERAL STRATEGIES

COMBAT MISSIONS

ECONOMIC MISSIONS

MULTIPLAYER

MAPS

Objectives

Acquire Weapons: 20 Bows

Acquire Weapons: 20 Crossbows

Acquire Weapons: 20 Spears

Acquire Weapons: 20 Pikes

This ancient forest is dying. The king needs yet more weapons. You have a limited time in which to deliver them.

You've got to try and establish a settlement in the middle of a forest in this mission, which is difficult because of the crowded stands of trees taking up all the ground area. Build the Saxon Hall in the clearing on the left side of the map, as shown in the figure below. Build the Granary nearby, but be careful to construct it in an area that is just barely big enough to fit its foundation. Save the larger areas for the construction of farms, which are tough to fit anywhere.

Employ a battalion of woodcutters early on (well, 4 or 5 of them anyway) to clear-cut the forest. You can worry about the environmental impact study later – in the short term, you've got to get some clearings made to accommodate the buildings in time to meet the time deadline in this mission. Build a Market with the initial wood supplies, which will help you meet

Tip

Real estate is very hard to come by in this mission – the trees take up all the room on the map! Make sure you are methodical in the building placement, using just enough room for each of the buildings and saving the larger open spaces for larger structures. Use the "flatten view" feature to maximize the efficiency.

the needs of the population if you can't get the own food industry started before the food stocks run out. After you have the woodcutters started, focus on feeding the people.

Once the settlement is self sufficient with food production, turn the attention to the construction of weapons buildings. You'll have to trade for iron, but you can sell many of the manufactured goods and products in the Market for profit. Weapons production is an expensive business, so don't stop growing the population as the mission progresses. A larger population means greater tax revenue, which gives you more buying power as the time crunch draws near. Also, don't be afraid to scrap the initial Woodcutter's Huts and move them out to the border of the forest as they progress, to maximize their cutting efficiency. In this scenario, the wood they produce is not nearly as important as the clear-cutting itself, to make room for the growth of the settlement. By the game's end, you should have several of each kind of weapon smith in operation, pumping out the required totals of goods. Don't forget an Armory to store them in, and by the end of the time limit you should have the quota filled for a mission victory.

THE TYRANT

Objectives

Achieve Population: 75

Achieve Fear Factor: Cruel (5)

Maintain a maximum fear factor for the given duration to prove you are the cruelest master in the land.

Cruelty breeds productivity, and you're out to prove it in this interesting mission. The challenge lies in maintaining popularity despite the resentment the draconian code of laws and outrageous punishments will inspire. This mission allows the malicious side to show through, with Chopping Blocks, Stockades, and even The Rack to maintain the rule with an iron fist. Build everything you can to raise the fear factor to its maximum capacity. Remember that Bad Things are not location sensitive, so put them all out in the far corners of the island.

Place the keep somewhat out of the way, to save space in the lower valleys for farms. Soon after the mission starts, select the Lord and have him take care of the bear, which will rampage through the settlement if left unchecked. There are plentiful resources on the island, so leave routes in between the buildings that will allow the workers to travel back to the stockpile efficiently.

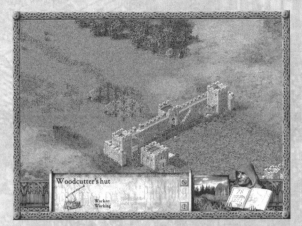

The popularity will take a beating from the target cruelty rating, so you'll have to plan on other popularity-enhancing methods from the beginning. Increased rations, religion, a healthy supply of Ale in the Inns, and even tax breaks can help you maintain the loyalty of the subjects despite the ever-present threat of death at the hands of the executioner.

Since the peasants will work harder at their jobs under the oppression, you can count on increased productivity from the food industries, which will help you maintain increased rations. The Priests will also work harder to bless the subjects, and the Brewery maids will even speed along the fermentation process (or cut corners in quality control – that's for you to figure out). While you could use this increased productivity to allow you to build fewer buildings for the same production levels, you should instead build the same amount of industry you normally would, and get more goods produced instead. You can use money to bolster the popularity, as well. With the rich resources available on the island, you can sell the goods at the market, and then use the money to pay the peasants a small allowance (or bribe) for their services.

Remember to grow the industries as you grow the population to the required level of 85. As the population grows, so too will the scale of the popularity-enhancing needs. More priests will be needed, more food required, and more money demanded in order to maintain the same levels of indulgence you are using to prop up the popularity. Grow them proportionately, and you'll be all set to claim a tyrannical victory at the end of the mission.

FREE BUILD MAPS

The free build maps allow you to build the castles of the dreams in several varied terrain types without any concern for mission objectives, enemy attacks or time limits. Without any such restrictions, you are free to grow the settlement into a mighty stronghold at the leisure. You must still provide for the economic welfare of the settlement, so the game is still quite challenging. Some of the maps also present you with advanced challenges, making these missions far from a walk in the park. Be sure to save the creations for appreciation at a later date!

FERNHAVEN

There are no winning conditions or attacks. What kind of castle can you create?

Fernhaven was host to an ancient settlement, now long since abandoned to the wind and rain. The remnants of the old structures are still visible in the upper portion of the central valley, and what was good enough for the ancients of ten is good enough for you! Consider placing the keep near this area, as it offers an excellent open ground for castle building. Quarry stone is available in the northwest, and substantial iron ore deposits line the southwestern hills, perfect for the assembly of a mighty garrison. Pitch can be pulled from the swamps in the south.

You may wish to start with a small Saxon Hall on the prominent bluff overlooking the central valley to the northeast. Once cleared of trees by the woodcutters, this hilltop offers an excellent defensive position, and its ramparts could afford a great deal of protection to the settlement in the valley below. Outer walls surrounding the lower settlement would further increase the security. Once completed, such a fortification could be nigh invincible to conventional attack.

FORK IN THE RIVER

The ancients of ten used rivers as a natural defense. Do the same on this wide-open valley.

The western side of this map hosts the greatest concentration of natural resources for you to exploit, so consider placing the initial keep on the left side of the map. There is quite a bit of room available on the northern side of the river, while the southern side offers a more elongated area for building the castle. Whichever you choose, remember to keep the future positions of the castle walls in mind as you build the initial settlement. It's better to plan for castle walls in advance, rather than being forced to delete buildings later to make room for them.

Resources of every kind abound at the Fork in the River. The southwestern corner of the map contains ample sources of pitch, while the rock pile in the northwest is well suited to multiple Quarries. You can find wood wherever you go, and the fertile river plain will grow any kind of crop you wish to plant. As with all free build missions, there are no enemy attacks.

GRASSLANDS

Build the castle of the dreams in these wide-open spaces. Resource rich, these fertile plains allow you to build the ultimate castle.

The Grasslands map affords you the opportunity to build what could be the largest, most elaborate castle in all of Stronghold. Resources abound on this map, and the unbroken, level ground allows for a truly massive structure. Consider building the keep near the cluster of trees in the middle of the map. This will place the Stockpile in a central location on the map, equidistant from the stone in the northeast, the pitch in the northwest, and the iron in the southwest.

Set the woodcutters to work immediately on the nearby trees. Eventually, you'll want these cleared to make room for the settlement, and the close proximity to the early keep makes for quick production. You may wish to sketch a plan for the dream castle early on, so that you have an overall idea before laying out the farms and industry. Alternately, you can choose to "build on the fly," adapting the plan to the needs as they arise.

However you do it, plan for the walls early on. You may wish to start with wooden palisades to offer early protection, and improve the defenses with stone later on. Naturally, you never have to worry about invasion in a free build mission, but it is fun to keep defensive considerations in mind anyway. Also, consider using concentric rings of walls to allow a staged defense of the mighty fortress. Be sure to save the game along the way, so you can come back another day and admire the creation!

THE ISLAND CASTLE

> Use the contours of this rock mount to recreate an island fortress, such as St. Michael located off the coast of France.

The Island Castle map is one of the more challenging free build maps because of the limited land area available for building. In particular, you'll find it very difficult to place food buildings on the map, making food supply a heavy concern on the island. Instead of trying to produce everything you need locally, consider relying on trade to feed the subjects. Export some of the island's riches such as iron and pitch, or sell manufactured goods like weapons and armor. Use the proceeds to buy food, and you should still end up ahead economically.

Place the Granary in the center of the island, and build a few Hunter's Posts next to it. The hunters can reach most of the island from its center. There is a small area of grasslands on the east side of the island, next to the beach. This area can host two Wheat Farms initially, and more when the woodcutters clear out the forest. Build a single Mill near the Stockpile, and supplement it with three Bakeries between the Granary and Stockpile. You will not find an open space large enough to host Dairy Farms on the island, and Apple Orchards don't yield enough food to make them worthwhile. With the above food production, you can at least support the early population without importing food.

Once you are feeding the subjects reliably, concentrate on export markets. Get the Pitch Rigs and Iron Mines operating, and build a marketplace in which to sell their products. Since you don't want to buy food every other minute, build another Granary when the population grows, to hold large quantities of food. This will afford you long periods to concentrate on building the castle, in between trading sessions at the market. At this point, you should be well established economically, and the island fortress of the dreams is only a matter of time. Build the Quarries and Ox Tethers to begin stone production, and start building the mighty walls.

WATERFALL VALLEY

Waterfall Valley is a pristine and resource-rich area. Establish a castle to match the area's beauty.

This map is extremely rich in ore and stone deposits, but its cramped spaces can present a challenge. The central valley is really the only viable candidate for hosting a castle of any reasonable size, so place the keep and Granary there. There are many natural resources on the northern and southern edges of the map, and you shouldn't have cause to cross the river.

The fertile valleys on this map can host any kind of farming you wish, so take advantage of this by building diversified food industries. A large bread industry will support a massive population, but remember to plan for crop blights by building other kinds of food industries, or by maintaining a reserve of flour. The larger population allows you to support a bigger castle. The varied terrain on this map can challenge you to be very creative in the construction, so if you're up to the challenge, see if you can make good use of the lay of the land to work to the military advantage.

Chapter 8

MULTIPLAYER GAMES

Stronghold's multiplayer mode gives you the opportunity to test your medieval mettle against other would-be lords in no-holds barred, head-to-head battles for supremacy. A wide variety of maps offer several different game styles, from all-out rushes on open maps to more civilized long-term games with strong starting fortresses. In addition to one-on-one battles, Stronghold can accommodate up to eight players at a time…for eight times the carnage.

GAME TYPES

There are two basic multiplayer game types: open maps and walled keeps. The following sections give you essential strategies for winning at each one. If you are playing with more than two players, make sure you hound some of them to join your side. Allies can be very powerful in a multiplayer game, as they work together not only militarily, but also symbiotically through trade and commerce.

OPEN MAPS

Maps with nothing more than keeps to start are outright footraces to see who can build troops first. Building fortifications in these games is usually too expensive and time consuming, when the enemy can have infantry in your settlement before your walls are complete. If you really feel you have time, try building a basic stockade and Wooden Gatehouse around your keep, to help you survive early attacks. Try not to let this effort delay your progress towards recruiting troops however, as this is of primary importance.

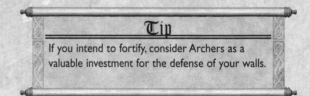

Tip
If you intend to fortify, consider Archers as a valuable investment for the defense of your walls.

Try to harass your opponent's settlement as soon as possible, to set him off balance as he tries to muster his forces. The loss of even one farm in the first few minutes of a game can have a staggering effect on an economy, and if you can get ahead of the power curve, you can bet on an eventual victory.

WALLED KEEPS

If you'd like to pursue a longer game, try one of the maps that gives each player a walled keep at the beginning of the game. This prevents an enemy force from winning the game with just a few Spearmen running amuck. With the threat of early annihilation removed, players can dedicate their attentions to more long-term goals, and you'll eventually see larger battles and sieges.

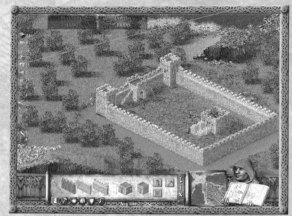

In these battles, seek to expand your walls early on, so that you have multiple rings of defense. It may be a good idea to use the edge of the screen as one of your walls if you can, to give you a great deal of "rear area" for farms, industry, and the like without having to maintain a complete wall.

MULTIPLAYER STRATEGIES

Multiplayer games play somewhat differently than the single player missions, because you are building a stronghold on the same map as your opponent. In the single player missions, you were either defending your stronghold against an invading army, or taking your own army to battle against an enemy fortress. In multiplayer games, your castles are competing for the very same resources. You are never truly at peace, as the enemy can strike at any time and with very little warning.

Do what you can to claim the resources for your own. Walling in key resources is an obvious way to gain exclusive access, but you can also use towers built within missile range of resources you would like to claim as your own. Station war engines or Archers atop the battlements of these towers, and destroy any enemy industries foolish enough to set up within your range.

RAIDING AND FEINTING

Attacking the enemy early on can be a very successful strategy, especially if you destroy key industries. In the early game, wood is the most important resource type for building, expansion, and defense. If you manage to destroy all of the enemy Woodcutters' Huts when the enemy has no reserves of wood, you can severely impact

Tip

Dealing with any attack takes time, even one in which the enemy has no chance of winning. This is why random attacks are useful. The enemy must stop what he is doing to go assess the attack and respond appropriately. While the opponent is distracted, the attacker may move other units with relative ease.

your enemy's ability to make war. Without adequate wood stocks, your opponent will not be able to produce new buildings, critical for successful expansion.

Human players are also easier to manipulate than the computer player. Try feints with small attack forces to draw their attention to one area, and then hammer them with a stronger main effort somewhere else on the map. The computer can take care of multiple challenges at once, but we humans can only look at one part of the map at a time! Use this to your advantage in your attacks.

Creeping

In a long game, you may find the enemy defenses are much to strong for you to overcome. Consider using incremental building steps, to get your walls up close to theirs, where you can support an attack from your very own towers. Simply construct towers along your route of advance, marching them ever closer to the enemy stronghold. Once you have the enemy wall in range, place a war engine in your furthest tower and take potshots at the wall and the defenders there.

SIEGES

Stronghold comes into its own with multiplayer sieges. Most strongholds will not be able to fit all of their industries (especially food industries) into their walls, forcing some structures out into the uncontrolled no-mans land. The enemy can lay siege to your castle, raising the buildings outside your walls in an attempt to starve you out of the fortress. Tunnelers can do their dastardly work while both economies grind on, with the besieged economy presumably grinding the most uncomfortably.

Don't forget to employ this tactic. Sometimes, simply destroying all of a Lord's outbuildings is enough to starve him out. When that happens, you can conquer an entire stronghold without firing so much as a shot at the garrison.

MULTIPLAYER MAPS

Below, you'll find detailed strategic notes on each of the multiplayer maps that come with Stronghold. Each map has its own unique set of challenges, and you should try to learn each one inside and out if you want to be truly successful in your rule. Don't waste time looking for where a certain resource is when you're facing an enemy army that's preparing faster than you are. Get to know these maps with the coverage below, and then prepare to claim victory on each one!

8 PLAYER – NO WALLS

This gigantic map is just like a track meet: 8 players, dashing to be the first to create an army. Without so much as a wooden palisade around the keeps, everyone is vulnerable to an early attack. One way to extend the game is to set the starting troops to Many. As contrary as that sounds, ensuring all players can defend themselves actually lends the game a bit of stability, reducing the impact of the first operational Barracks.

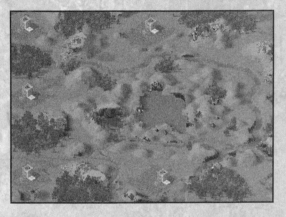

Get an ally on this map if you're playing with several people. It's very important to have at least one secure border. Each keep has immediate access to its own small source of stone and iron very nearby, with the deposits for the players on the right side and upper right corner sharing the same hill. These players should be allied, if teams are being used, as they will come into immediate conflict otherwise.

Pitch is available in massive quantities at the center of the map, and peasants headed to and from work may need military escort if they are expected to return safely. One tactic is to make a play for control of the pitch by placing a tower overlooking the swamp. Defend it well, for your enemies will be hungry for pitch. If you'd rather stay out of the whole competition for access to the swamp, simply trade for your pitch at the Marketplace.

8 PLAYER MAYHEM

This map is exactly the same as the other 8-player map, although the starting orientation is rotated clockwise 90 degrees. As with all of the other maps, each player starts with a walled keep, guaranteeing security in the early and mid game. The players on the left and upper left have a slight advantage due to the added defensibility of the rivers, but the effect is negligible overall.

Some of the Gatehouses are oriented inconveniently for access to the corresponding stone and iron deposits. Feel free to open a small hole in your wall early on, to be replaced later on with a new gatehouse. Consider extending your walls as soon as possible to cover your resources, guaranteeing you a source of goods for use or trade. If you conquer one of your neighbors and the game is going into overtime, incorporate the old castle into your own defenses!

BUTTERFLY ISLAND

This island scenario hosts four equally viable positions on their own small fingers of an island. The combat is funneled into the middle of the island, since it is the only land bridge between the opposing strongholds. This should allow for relatively robust castle construction, since you can maximize your defenses along a single axis, while your rear remains completely secure. On the other hand, a failure of your defenses means a critical blow, so make sure to employ multiple lines of walls.

Station your initial troops near the neck of your finger of the island to guard your settlement as it grows. If your neighbors are aggressive, build a wooden wall early on, and add a few platforms or even a tower to bolster your defenses. Focus on the long run, and build a strong economy, relying on the natural defensive properties of your position to see you through the early stage of the game. Once your economy is established, turn your attentions to weapon and troop production, and out-produce your enemies. Try to take on only one enemy at a time, and work on a quick and decisive end to their settlement once you decide to attack. As soon as you've eliminated an opponent, consolidate your victory by building a forward wall to protect both sections of the island.

KING OF THE HILL

Playing on this map can be one of the most enjoyable experiences in the game. Each player starts with a nearly invincible position on a fertile isthmus, connected by a very narrow land bridge to the central hill and the other players. A fully protected keep complete with moat ensures early safety, and the addition of a large gatehouse at the front of the isthmus will ensure security over the course of the entire game.

The object is to storm the central keep and hold onto it, giving you control of the hill. Every moment you are in control of the hill, you score points. By clicking on the crown at the beginning of the game, you can select the number of points needed for victory. Whoever accumulates the required number of points first, wins. Be sure to keep track of the point levels of your opponents.

If one of your enemies is nearing victory, all other players should mount a last-ditch attack to try and depose him, or else the game will end in that player's victory. Although you'll want to contribute to this effort, you must also try to preserve a little something for yourself after the dust settles. The trick is to contribute to the effort to stave off defeat without bearing the brunt of the work. Deploy your troops with tactical precision in order to do this, preserving them for the inevitable second fight that follows after the old king is dethroned.

MOUNTAIN FORTRESS

This two-player map provides players with an excellent historical feel. Each Lord begins with a mature castle situated atop an imposing hill. The strongholds overlook fertile valleys, which will likely host farms. The river is surrounded by a dike, and effectively separates the two fiefdoms. However, the river is fordable along its entire length, so it is a non-factor, as the enemy can cross over into your territory at will.

Stone and iron are abundant on the hills that sit on the far side of each player's domain. Curiously, the player on the right has no access to pitch on his side of the river. The closest pitch is right next to the enemy's stone and iron deposits. The player on the right can either trade for pitch, or make a play for control of the resources on the left side of the screen. In the latter case, you'll probably end up going to war fairly early on, because the pitch is located so close to the enemy's resources.

NEED AN ALLY?

This interesting map has no stone resources, leaving you with wooden walls as your only option for defense. All of the map's resources lie in the middle of the map, ensuring a great deal of conflict. As the name of the map implies, an ally will make it easier to ensure access to the resources, and this map is very likely to foster armies fighting in the field rather than over castles.

Even though you are working with wood, castle design is no different than standard stone castles. You should still endeavor to construct a defense in depth, with two or more concentric rings

of wooden walls. Once your economy is thriving, you may choose to trade for stone, depending on your evaluation of the enemy threat to your keep. If the battle is in the field, focus on mustering troops. Still, even a stone tower behind wooden walls will help you in the defense.

THE FOUR CASTLES

This four-player map is an ideal setting for a classical struggle between four Lords. Each castle has full access to all resource types, with stone and iron being located on the four tiny islands in the middle of the map. Concentrate on force projection by mustering an effective army, because the islands are vulnerable to enemy attack, and losing your Iron Mines and Quarries can be crippling.

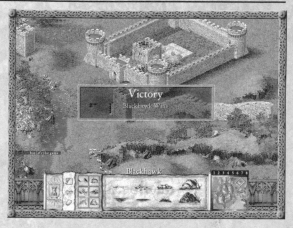

You can extend your castle out towards the islands to offer missile coverage to your industries, which will help ensure their survival. Unfortunately, this also puts your missile troops in range of the enemy resources, which may be seen as a hostile move. If you are playing with a full map, see if

you can establish a truce or a treaty with one of the other Lords, and concentrate your efforts on one of your hostile neighbors. As with any other multiplayer game, try not to make multiple enemies at the same time.

THE TACTICIAN

This map features two incredibly defensible positions, and will lead to some of the most epic sieges seen in the game if played well. Both players have their backs to the wall, allowing each of you to concentrate your defenses on your front facing. There are ample resources of all kinds on this map, with an expansive no-man's land in between the castles. Consider ambushing your enemy with Archers from the heights if he advances through the middle ground; counter this tactic with Knights to run down the Archers.

Make sure you have at least two rings of defenses around your keep. There is little room to extend the walls outward, but you have some leeway in the internal construction of your castle. Flat ground is at a premium, however, so you must plan your building efforts carefully. Note that since you are on the edge of the map, these defensive rings can actually be semicircles or even horseshoes, allowing you to fit more industry inside your castle. Make sure you provide for the food needs of your population with enough farms, most of which will have to go inside your walls.

WALL TO WALL

Four castles share this map, which is dominated by plains. Each castle is fairly mature, with a few towers around the walls and two Gatehouses providing easy access to private reserves of resources for each player. The map is called "Wall to Wall" because it's fairly easy for the castles to extend into one another, creating the somewhat comical possibility of tower-to-tower sniping competitions from the comfort of your own castle!

With such close quarters, it's important to claim as much territory as you can for yourself. Try to reinforce your position and strengthen your claim to your precious resources by walling off your starting corner. Even a wooden wall to start with is good, as it signifies your claim to the land, and allows you to defend it with some measure of success. As your economy grows, build towers to support your claims, and install war engines atop them. You may wish to try for an "iron ring" approach of towers around your lands, with interlocking fields of fire for mutual support.

Chapter 9

MAPS

This section will have complete maps of every available scenario in the game. Take advantage of these maps and use them to decimate the enemy be it computer or human. Take the fight to them or hole up in a well-defended corner. This is where the planning ends, and the true strategizing begins.

COMBAT CAMPAIGN

GATHERING THE LOST

FINISHING THE FORT

ELIMINATING THE WOLVES

THE HIDDEN LOOKOUT

BETWEEN A ROCK AND A HARD PLACE

THE RAT'S PROPOSAL

BREAKING THE SIEGE

BASICS

CHARACTERS

STRUCTURES

GENERAL STRATEGIES

COMBAT MISSIONS

ECONOMIC MISSIONS

MULTIPLAYER

MAPS

DEALING WITH THE DEVIL

THE RAT'S LAST STAND

THE SNAKE HUNT BEGINS

FIRST BLOOD

THE RANSOM

SNAKE EYES

THE MOUNTAIN PASS

CARVING A PATH

FIGHTING RETREAT

SMOKEY BACON

END OF THE PIG

PENNING IN THE WOLF

MUCH WAILING AND GNASHING OF TEETH

FINAL VENGEANCE

SIEGE MISSIONS

CASTELL Y BERE

GLUECKSBURG

BASICS

CHARACTERS

STRUCTURES

GENERAL STRATEGIES

COMBAT MISSIONS

ECONOMIC MISSIONS

MULTIPLAYER

MAPS

BASICS CHARACTERS STRUCTURES GENERAL STARTEGIES COMBAT MISSIONS ECONOMIC MISSIONS MULTIPLAYER MAPS

GUADAMUR

HEIDELBERG

190

JAVIER

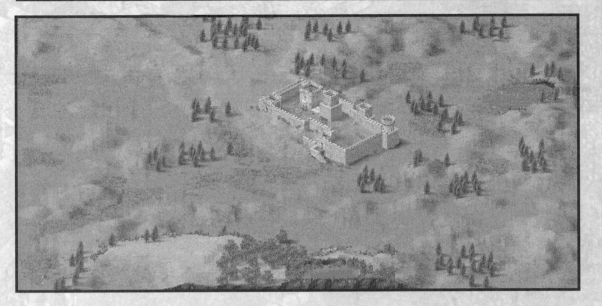

LEEDS

BASICS

CHARACTERS

STRUCTURES

GENERAL STRATEGIES

COMBAT MISSIONS

ECONOMIC MISSIONS

MULTIPLAYER

MAPS

MONTERIGGIONI

WARTBURG

WINDSOR

INVASION MISSIONS

DEFENDING THE HOMELAND

BASICS
CHARACTERS
STRUCTURES
GENERAL STRATEGIES
COMBAT MISSIONS
ECONOMIC MISSIONS
MULTIPLAYER
MAPS

THE FAT PIG (OINK, OINK)

THE RAT'S REVENGE

THE VIPER'S NEST

THE WEAK, THE BAD, THE FAT, AND THE SLIPPERY

WHO'S AFRAID OF THE BIG BAD WOLF?

ECONOMICS CAMPAIGN

VICTORY FEAST

THE LONG VALLEY

GATHERING THE HARVEST

A DETERRENT

A CASTLE IN THE MARSH

ECONOMICS MISSIONS

A REQUEST FROM THE KING

BLESSING THE PEASANTS

BASICS

CHARACTERS

STRUCTURES

GENERAL STARTEGIES

COMBAT MISSIONS

ECONOMIC MISSIONS

MULTIPLAYER

MAPS

THE EMERGING CITY

THE FOREST

THE TYRANT

FREE BUILD MISSIONS

FERNHAVEN

FORK IN THE RIVER

GRASSLANDS

THE ISLAND CASTLE

WATERFALL VALLEY

BASICS

CHARACTERS

STRUCTURES

GENERAL STARTEGIES

COMBAT MISSIONS

ECONOMIC MISSIONS

MULTIPLAYER

MAPS

MULTIPLAYER

8 PLAYER - NO WALLS

8 PLAYER MAYHEM

BUTTERFLY ISLAND

KING OF THE HILL

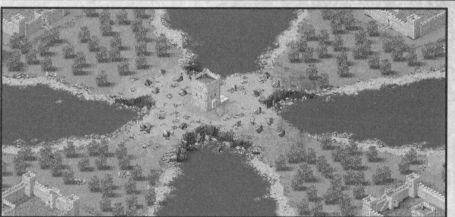

MOUNTAIN FORTRESS

BASICS
CHARACTERS
STRUCTURES
GENERAL STRATEGIES
COMBAT MISSIONS
ECONOMIC MISSIONS
MULTIPLAYER
MAPS

NEED AN ALLY?

THE FOUR CASTLES

THE TACTICIAN

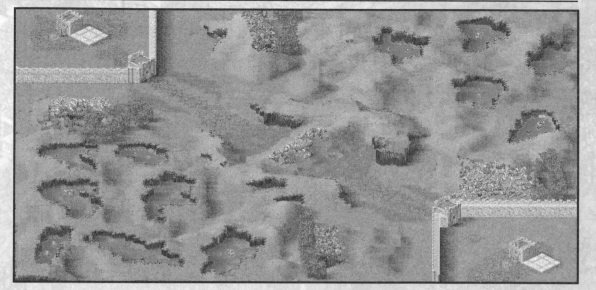

WALL TO WALL

THE NEW CARIBBEAN **DICTATOR** SIM FROM
THE MAKERS OF RAILROAD TYCOON 2™!

TROPICO

You rule.

"The most unique and intriguing
strategy game of the new year" –*PC Gamer*

TEEN
T
CONTENT RATED BY
ESRB

AVAILABLE AT YOUR LOCAL RETAILER!